SCHOOL COUNSELOR'S LETTER BOOK

KENNETH W. HITCHNER
ANNE TIFFT-HITCHNER
E. ANDRE APOSTOL

THE CENTER FOR APPLIED
RESEARCH IN EDUCATION

Library of Congress Cataloging-in-Publication Data

Hitchner, Kenneth W.
    School counselor's letter book / Kenneth W. Hitchner, Anne Tifft-
Hitchner, E. Andre Apostol.
      p. cm.
    ISBN 0-87628-786-0
    1. Student counselors—United States.   2. Letter-writing.
I. Tifft-Hitchner, Anne.   II. Apostol, E. Andre.   III. Center for
Applied Research in Education.   IV. Title.
LB1027.5.H59   1991   91-526
371.4—dc20   CIP

Printed in the United States of America

10   9   8

ISBN 0-87628-786-0

**THE CENTER FOR APPLIED RESEARCH
IN EDUCATION**

On the World Wide Web at http://www.phdirect.com

ABOUT THE AUTHORS ———————————

Kenneth W. Hitchner is the author of a *Survival Guide for the Secondary School Counselor* and a co-author of *Making a Difference in College Admission* (The Center for Applied Research in Education, 1987, 1989). He received his B.A. degree in English and social studies from Dickinson College, Carlisle, PA. After doing graduate work in school counseling at Bucknell University, he went on to earn Ed.M. and Ed.S. degrees in school administration from Rutgers University. Mr. Hitchner has twenty-eight years of school counseling experience, working in three different New Jersey school districts prior to his arrival at East Brunswick High School. The author and lecturer spent eight years as director of counseling. He is a past vice president of the New Jersey School Counselor Association and has been published in the *Journal of College Admissions,* the College Board's *College Prep,* and the *New Jersey Reporter.*

Anne Tifft-Hitchner is a co-author of *Making a Difference in College Admission.* She is the recipient of a B.A. degree from Georgian Court College, Lakewood, NJ, and an M.A. degree in philosophy of science from St. John's University, Queens, NY. She has taught students in middle school through junior college, doing most of her teaching at East Brunswick High School in the content areas of chemistry and physics. The author has also taught English at The Peddie School in Hightstown, NJ. Ms. Tifft-Hitchner has served extensively as a student advisor, both at the high school and college levels.

E. Andre Apostol is co-author of the manual, *A Counselor/Teacher Resource Guide for Sex Fair Counseling and Guidance* (Rutgers University Press, 1978). He received his B.S. degree in education from Seton Hall University, South Orange, NJ, and earned his M.A. degree in student personnel services from Kean College, Union, NJ. Mr. Apostol obtained his School Psychologist certification from Rider College, Lawrenceville, NJ. His twenty-four years of experience as an educator includes elementary classroom teaching and counseling at the elementary, secondary, and adult levels. The author is an adjunct professor at Kean College and has served as regional coordinator for the American School Counselor Association (ASCA).

ABOUT THIS RESOURCE _____

In all too many schools across the nation, counselors are drowning in paperwork. The *School Counselor's Letter Book* can be your life preserver. It places in your hands over 220 highly effective, counselor-tested model letters, memoranda, forms, programs, policy statements, information sheets, and more, to help save you time and effort in four general areas:

- Counseling for Educational Development
- Personal Counseling
- Counseling for the Future
- Communication and Professional Development

These four areas are further subdivided into sixteen topics that cover all aspects of your job, from *Course Selection and Programming* to *Crisis Issues*.

You can easily adapt any of these models to your own particular situation; some can be photocopied for immediate use. If you already have a similar piece in your files, this book may help you improve it. And, a quick look through this book may also furnish you with fresh ideas for many situations.

The *School Counselor's Letter Book* offers you a chance to find out what successful school counselors at both the elementary and secondary levels are doing and how they do it. You will find forms that streamline administrative tasks, information sheets that answer the most common questions from students and parents, and memos and letters of all kinds that you can use to build communication and rapport with colleagues and clients. You will also find ready-to-use policy statements that have proven to be effective in schools across the country and a unique collection of materials to guide students, parents—and you!—through the complete college admissions process.

HOW TO USE THIS RESOURCE ⸺

To find a particular letter or form, simply locate the most applicable topic in the table of contents and scan the list for the title of the piece you need. Since so much of what a school counselor does is "seasonal" in nature, the letters and forms have been arranged in chronological order where appropriate. There is a mix of material for both elementary and secondary counselors; choose the piece most suitable for your age-level, or adapt an item to suit your needs.

We hope that this book will permit you to more effectively and efficiently perform the many important roles of a school counselor.

Kenneth W. Hitchner

Anne Tifft-Hitchner

E. Andre Apostol

ACKNOWLEDGMENTS _____

We are grateful to the following people for their encouragement and special assistance in the preparation of this book:

At East Brunswick: the Board of Education; JoAnn Magistro, Assistant Superintendent of Schools; Charles King, Principal of East Brunswick High School; Frank LoPresti, Guidance Department Chair; Rocco Magliozzi, Special Education Chair; and the counselors, especially Robert Sullivan, Career Specialist.

Our appreciation to the following colleagues who also provided support for and valuable input into the writing of the text: David Peterson, Watchung Hills Regional High School, Warren, NJ; Thomas Brown, Port Clinton High School, OH; Tassie Livingston, Madison High School, NJ; James Alexander, Jr., Highland Park High School, IL; Frances Feldman, Middlesex High School, NJ; Gerald Bell, Edison Township Public Schools, NJ; Arthur G. Barnes, Cedar Ridge High School, Old Bridge, NJ; Lillian Werenne, Gilmore Fisher Junior High School, Ewing Township, NJ; Evelyn White and Karl Riemann, Hamilton Township Public Schools, NJ; Robert W. Ferris, Diane Waronka, and Joanne Johnson, Cherry Hill Public Schools, NJ.

Particular thanks, too, to Sandra Hutchison, our editor, for her fine counsel and continuous encouragement.

QUICK OVERVIEW OF CONTENTS _____

The actual table of contents, with page numbers, follows this listing.

SECTION I. COUNSELING FOR EDUCATIONAL DEVELOPMENT

Topic 1.   Course Selection and Programming
Topic 2.   Homework and Study Habits
Topic 3.   Progress Reports and Warnings
Topic 4.   Exceptional Students
Topic 5.   Testing and Curriculum

SECTION II. PERSONAL COUNSELING

Topic 6.   Developmental Counseling
Topic 7.   Behavior and Self-Esteem
Topic 8.   Recognition Activities
Topic 9.   Crisis Issues
Topic 10. Attendance and Transfers

SECTION III. COUNSELING FOR THE FUTURE

Topic 11. Postsecondary Planning
Topic 12. College Admissions

SECTION IV. COMMUNICATION AND PROFESSIONAL DEVELOPMENT

Topic 13. Conferences
Topic 14. Communicating with Teachers
Topic 15. Communicating with Parents and the Community
Topic 16. Evaluation and Accountability

CONTENTS _____

Topic 2. Homework and Study Habits • 25

Topic 3. Progress Reports and Warnings • 48

SECTION III. COUNSELING FOR THE FUTURE • 148

Topic 11. Postsecondary Planning • 148

Topic 12. College Admissions • 166

SECTION IV. COMMUNICATION AND PROFESSIONAL DEVELOPMENT • 216

Topic 13. Conferences • 216

Topic 14. Communicating with Teachers • 224

I. Counseling for Educational Development _____

Educational development counseling permeates almost everything you do. You can see it in your work with the gifted and talented, the underachiever, the collegebound, and the special education student. It is at least implicit in your dealings with troubled students, administrators/supervisors, and other staff personnel.

A counselor's advising time is sometimes spent trying to "show the way" toward completion of homework assignments. (Note that a significant number of the entries in this section relate to the homework/study issue.) Counselors recognize that a student's problem in not turning in assignments is often an aspect of underachievement. Students have to see the problem for what it is: They are doing serious damage to their sense of self-worth, to say nothing of what they are doing to their grades. The counselor's challenge is to help the student improve his or her stance. And what a challenge it is! Bringing the underachiever around is one of the most difficult of counseling tasks. Since repeated, unsuccessful attempts can become part of the problem, it can be valuable for you to find out how other staff members have tried to attack the situation.

At times you may have to resort to doing "contract" work: placing the underachieving student under contract, a process whereby student, parent, and counselor agree on certain short-term improvement goals. This type of program is found most often at the elementary level, where the formulation of sound study habits is crucial.

Another significant aspect of this type of counseling is assisting students with subject-choice issues, i.e., course selection and the design of a program of studies for subsequent academic years. Placing students in *appropriate* courses, according to abilities, interests, values, and career aspirations, is one of the most *serious and vital responsibilities of the school counselor.*

Classroom teachers are wonderful sources of information. Both you and your students would do well to tap into this rich supplemental source of input on what to take and when and for a more detailed analysis of certain courses. As counselors, we probably "lean on" teachers most heavily in the subject-matter area.

The documents in this section should also make it easier for you to cope with such other issues as compensatory education, graduation, performance reports, and retention.

1. COURSE SELECTION AND PROGRAMMING

Who Has the Power of Placement?

Principals sometimes think that counselors are too passive in their dealings with students and parents; that they are afraid to take a hard line. This issue is raised especially when it comes to placing a student in a particular course or course level. In an attempt to raise educational standards, many school systems have instituted course and grade prerequisites that can limit the options open to you and your counselee. If you plan to vary from the accepted norm, you should be prepared to both state *and record* your position.

On the other hand, if a principal grants *you* "power of placement," then he needs to support your decisions. It is imperative to learn where you stand on this particular issue.

■   ■   ■

Orientation Meeting Notice

Date: _____

Dear Parent/Guardian:

An orientation meeting for parents whose children will be entering the _____ grade next year will be held on _____ at _____ P.M. in the _____. All aspects of the school curriculum will be discussed.

We look forward to meeting with you at that time.

Sincerely,

_____
Roberta Warren
Counselor

Orientation Letter

Date: _____

Dear Parents of Fifth Graders:

This September your youngster will begin attending Frank Burton Middle School. It is most important that together we develop an appropriate program of studies for him/her. A series of parent orientation programs has been scheduled for later this month to help accomplish this objective.

Enclosed is a packet of materials that describes next year's courses, including electives. It would be beneficial for you to read and discuss these materials with your youngster prior to attending the orientation session. Special attention should be paid to the selection of elective courses.

Your meeting will be held on _____ at _____. Please mark your calendar accordingly. You might want to bring the enclosed packet of information with you to the meeting.

I look forward to seeing you!

　　　　　　　　　　　　　　　 Sincerely yours,

　　　　　　　　　　　　　　　 _____

　　　　　　　　　　　　　　　 George Win
　　　　　　　　　　　　　　　 Counselor

Orientation Letter with Course Offerings

Date: _____

Dear Parents/Guardians of Fifth Graders:

This fall your youngster will be attending Hillsdale Middle School as a sixth grader. Enclosed is a packet of materials that explains the entire course selection process, including available electives.

Required core courses include: reading, English, mathematics, science, social studies, and physical education. Required cycle courses include: health, computers, art, and technology. Students take each of these cycle courses for one marking period.

Your youngster will also have the opportunity to select *two* electives. You and he/she will want to give careful consideration to the selection of these subjects. The need for teachers, materials, classroom space, and textbooks is to some extent based on your elective selections. Consequently, once you have made elective choices, we ask you to avoid making any changes unless a real emergency develops.

Elective choices are as follows: band, orchestra, chorus, music, art, technology, foreign language (Spanish, French, German, or Latin), and study skills. Again, *two* electives may be chosen.

The Counseling Department stands ready to help you and your youngster in this important decision-making process. Don't hesitate to contact us if you have further questions or concerns.

Cordially,

_____

Harold R. Akin
Counselor

Choice of Electives Form

STUDENT ————————————————— DATE —————————

I have read the statement on course selection and have discussed the choice of electives with my son/daughter. We have chosen the following electives:

(Please indicate your first and second choices by placing the numbers *1* and *2* in the appropriate spaces. You will be notified if there is any scheduling difficulty. Return this page to your homeroom teacher by ———————————————————.)

————— Band   Foreign languages:

————— Orchestra   ————— Spanish

————— Chorus   ————— French

————— Music   ————— German

————— Art   ————— Latin

————— Technology

————— Study Skills

Parent/Guardian's signature —————————————

Phone number —————————————

Extracurricular Offerings: Letter to Incoming Students

OCEAN VIEW HIGH SCHOOL
COUNSELING DEPARTMENT

Dear Incoming Student:

As the school year commences, we would like to remind you that Ocean View is more than a building full of laboratories and classrooms, just as education is more than a grade on a rcport card.

Your school is also the people who inhabit it, and your education is a mix of *all* of the experiences that you will encounter while attending Ocean View High School.

With these thoughts in mind, we would like to draw your attention to the fine array of extracurricular offerings that are provided for you. An actual list of clubs and activities can be found on page 40 of the Student Handbook, which will be mailed to you soon by the administration.

Club involvement can open up a whole world of pleasure and accomplishment. Such participation can pay big dividends. So, take full advantage of what the school has to offer. Become involved!

Best wishes for an enjoyable and productive school year!

The Counseling Department

Parent Orientation Night

A most interesting and productive way of reaching out to parents about curricular offerings is to offer a program in which subject-area chairpersons discuss offerings with parents. The very presence of subject-area experts provides the evening with a heightened sense of professionalism. Counselors can be on hand to introduce chairs and moderate each of the panels. Speakers should be given about seven minutes, and *no more,* to make presentations. This allows about ten minutes for audience questions at the end of each session. Allowing for a fifteen-minute general session and twenty minutes of hall-passing time, this fast-paced program should last about 2 ½ hours.

■　　■　　■

Parent Orientation Night Invitation

Date: _____

Dear Parents:

The Middleton High School Counseling Department cordially invites parents of eighth-grade students to the high school to discuss course selection for next year. Chairpersons from each subject-matter area will give a brief presentation; then, along with the counselors, they will try to answer any questions that you might have.

The meeting will be held on Thursday, January 15, in the high school auditorium. Prior to the meeting date, your youngster will receive a course selection guide. Ask him or her to share this guide with you, and then please bring it to the meeting.

We look forward to you joining us!

Sincerely,

_____
Robert Bradford
Director

Enclosure

Parent Orientation Night Program

WELCOME TO
MIDDLETON HIGH SCHOOL

7:30 P.M. MHS AUDITORIUM

7:30–7:45	GREETINGS: INTRODUCTION and GENERAL COMMENTS:	Principal Director of Counseling
7:50–8:20	Curriculum Session A—Auditorium:	Social Studies, Music, and Mathematics
8:25–8:55	Curriculum Session B—Cafeteria:	Home Economics, Art, and Industrial Arts
9:00–9:30	Curriculum Session C—Library:	English, Business, and Computer Studies
9:35–10:05	Curriculum Session D—Gymnasium:	Science, Foreign Languages, and Health and P.E.

LAST NAMES	7:50–8:20	8:25–8:55	9:00–9:30	9:35–10:05
A–F	A	B	C	D
G–L	B	C	D	A
M–R	C	D	A	B
S–Z	D	A	B	C

Placement Recommendations for Rising Sixth-Grade Students

The placement recommendation form, utilized by middle school counselors, is completed by teachers for rising sixth graders and by mathematics and reading specialists for rising seventh graders.

■   ■   ■

EAST BRUNSWICK PUBLIC SCHOOLS
HAMMARSKJOLD GUIDANCE DEPARTMENT

PLACEMENT RECOMMENDATIONS FOR GRADE 7

STUDENT NAME: _____

TEACHER: _____

Standardized Test Scores (National Percentiles):

Grade 5		Grade 6	
Total Reading	_____	Total Reading	_____
Total Language	_____	Total Language	_____
Total Math	_____	Total Math	_____
C.S.I. or I.Q.	_____	C.S.I. or I.Q.	_____

Report Card Grades: (See attached report card)

Placement Recommendations: (Circle one)

Reading — Advanced   Developmental   Remedial   Basic Skills
English — Advanced   Developmental   Remedial
Math   — Algebra I   Pre-Algebra   Math Enrichment
              Math Development   Basic Skills

Day One/Two Electives: (Check each column)

	First Choice	*Second Choice*
Technology		
Art Exploration		
Chorus		
Band		
Orchestra		

Foreign Language Electives: (Check each column)

	First Choice	*Second Choice*
Spanish		
French		
German		
Reading Enrichment		
Study Skills		

Special Considerations/Comments Regarding Placement: _____

Course Guide Introduction

Here is an excerpt from the front matter of an annually published course guide.

■   ■   ■

YOUR COUNSELOR AND YOU

You have been assigned a very special person to help you grow and develop during high school—your counselor. Your counselor's major task is to see that you graduate after having experienced a rich and rewarding high school career.

Yes, your counselor is the key figure who coordinates your efforts with those of your parents and teachers to enable you to realize your goals.

Help *is* available to you whenever you need it. All you need to do is to stop in the Counseling Office and request to see your counselor. From time to time he or she will be contacting you. Your meetings together may concern test results, grades, personal problems, post-high school plans, or any number of other issues that can arise from life at high school.

The proper selection of subject-matter courses is one of the most important tasks that you and your counselor accomplish together. Consider with care the many courses listed in this guide. Your counselor will do everything possible to help you select the most appropriate program of studies for the next academic year.

This guide has been prepared after much thought and investigation. It has been designed to meet the needs of all students. Read it carefully—notice that your school offers a wide variety of subject-matter choices, all of which are intended to educate you thoroughly.

Recommendation for Elective Developmental Courses

DATE: _____

TO: All Counselors
FROM: Walter Skirka, Chairman
RE: Programming of Developmental Reading and/or Composition

After discussing developmental programs, Mrs. Arenz, English Chairperson, and I decided that: If an English student has been recommended to receive additional support in reading and/or writing, the counselor should make sure that the student is informed of that recommendation and is *encouraged* to take this class as an elective subject.

We must remember that these courses are only being *recommended.* The final decision rests with the student and his or her parents.

Enclosed is a copy of the form that the English and Counseling Departments will utilize jointly.

STUDENT: _____ GRADE: _____
RECOMMENDING TEACHER: _____

Please rate the student's capability on a scale of 1 (low) to 5 (high).

Motivation and attitude toward learning
1   2   3   4   5

Ability to communicate effectively in writing
1   2   3   4   5

Ability to understand what he/she reads
1   2   3   4   5

Ability to analyze what he/she reads
1   2   3   4   5

Probable final grade: _____

I would / would not recommend additional support in reading.
    (circle one)

I would / would not recommend additional support in writing.
    (circle one)

Comments: _____

Teacher's Course Recommendation

In some school systems, teachers are directly involved in course selection. Here, mathematics teachers suggest to parents the proper math course for their youngsters to take during the following school year. It is a letter of which the counselor would, at the very least, want to be aware.

■   ■   ■

Date: _____

Dear Parent/Guardian:

Scheduling time is once again upon us, and we want to ensure that *all* students select a mathematics course appropriate to their abilities, interests, and aspirations. As _____ mathematics teacher, I recommend that he/she select _____ for the coming academic year.

We hope that you will consider this recommendation as you develop next year's program of studies with your son/daughter.

Sincerely,

_____
Teacher

Teacher-Recommended Course Level Change Form

An in-house form can be utilized by the classroom teacher to recommend a level change.

■   ■   ■

TEACHER-RECOMMENDED COURSE LEVEL CHANGE

STUDENT _____ GRADE _____

SUBJECT _____ CURRENT LEVEL _____

TEACHER _____ CLASS PERIOD _____

COUNSELOR _____

Class   _____

Test Scores   _____

                 _____

                 _____

Student's Class Average _____

Standardized Test Scores	*Grade Level*	*Percentile*
Reading	_____	_____
Language Arts	_____	_____
Mathematics	_____	_____

Teacher's Recommendations:

Subject-Area Supervisor: Approved _____ Not Approved _____

NOTE: Submit to Counseling Department.

Application for Advanced Placement Course

Some school forms do not directly impact on a counselor's role and function, but rather they have an indirect effect. Here is one of them—one that, for better or for worse, restricts entrance into AP English.

■   ■   ■

ADVANCED PLACEMENT ENGLISH APPLICATION

NAME: _____

ADDRESS: _____

TELEPHONE #: _____

10TH GR. ENGLISH TEACHER: _____

FINAL GRADE: _____

11TH GR. ENGLISH TEACHER: _____

MID-YR. GRADE: _____

NOTE: To be eligible to take Advanced Placement English, a student must maintain a B or better average in English 3 Honors or an A in Academic English 3.

OR

Sit for a written examination in order to demonstrate proficiency in interpretative reading and in writing.

The following requirements apply to *all* applicants:

1. On the reverse side of this application, please cite your reasons for wanting to take AP English. (Limit yourself to no more than 200 words.)
2. Those students who are admitted to the program will be expected to read extensively during the summer, maintain a reading log, and be prepared to discuss or write about the studied material at the opening of school.
3. Accepted students will be encouraged to take the AP English examination in May.

I HAVE READ AND UNDERSTAND THE ABOVE REQUIREMENTS.

_____   _____
Student Signature   Parent/Guardian Signature

Parent Approval for Skipping Lunch

Some students want to "take it all" when it comes to course selection—even to the point of skipping lunch. Certain states mandate that students be provided with a lunch period, and only the parents can waive such a requirement. Here's a form to keep it all legal, and one that should clear the counselor to more properly schedule the student.

■   ■   ■

TO: Anthony Reston, Principal

RE: Request for Omitting Lunch

I realize that for nutritional and educational reasons, the school does not recommend that students miss their lunch.

However, I believe that it would be in my child's, _____
(full name)

best interest to omit his/her lunch to take an additional course. I hereby give him/her permission to do so.

_____
Parent Signature

_____
Date

Pass/Fail Contract

Schools usually adopt pass/fail options for one or more of the following reasons: (1) to encourage students to "stretch" academically by pursuing challenging work that they might not otherwise pursue, e.g., a semester of calculus or the fourth year of a foreign language; (2) to encourage students to take courses outside of their strength areas; or (3) to relieve grade pressures in certain nonacademic and/or skills courses.

■   ■   ■

DATE: _____

TO: ALL STAFF AND STUDENTS

FROM: JOHN MILLER, ASSISTANT PRINCIPAL

RE: DETAILS OF PASS/FAIL OPTION

1. Students may elect to take one course each semester on a pass/fail basis. If a student elects a full-year course, no other course may be taken as pass/fail. Students *must* discuss this option with their counselors.

2. Once the pass/fail option has been elected, students MAY NOT request a change back to traditional letter grades.

3. Students will get course credit if they pass a particular course. Grades of P or F will not be included in the computation of the GPA and consequent class ranking.

4. Teachers will grade pass/fail students in the same manner as all other students but will issue only a P or F on a student's report card.

5. Those who opt for pass/fail AFTER a quarter in which letter grades were issued should have these letter grades changed to P/F through the teacher.

6. Students must indicate their preference to receive pass/fail grades according to the following calendar:

> Fall Semester Course 11/6
> Full-Year Course 12/20
> Spring Semester Course 3/27

NOTE: Application deadlines will be *strictly* adhered to.

(Pass/Fail Contract, continued)

. . . .

PASS FAIL CONTRACT

I hereby request to take (course) _____
for _____ (number of) credits on a Pass/Fail basis. I understand that once
I have elected the Pass/Fail option, I *may not* request that traditional letter grades be
recorded on official school records.

_____
Student's Name (PRINTED)

_____
Student's Signature

_____
Parent's Signature

_____
Teacher's Signature

_____   _____
Date   Counselor's Signature

NOTE: Upon completion, this form will be retained by your counselor.

Petition for Partial Senior Program

WATCHUNG HILLS REGIONAL HIGH SCHOOL
WARREN, NEW JERSEY

PETITION FOR PARTIAL SENIOR PROGRAM

STUDENT SECTION

I, the undersigned Watchung Hills Junior, respectfully petition the school administration for permission to substitute a yearlong activity (enrollment at a county or collegiate institution, employment, independent or correspondence study, or other specified, directed activity) for the normal 26-credit program. My proposal is as follows: (Describe in detail.)

If this request is approved, I agree to release the school from responsibility for me after I leave the school. I agree to leave the school grounds each day as soon as my school program is completed. I will inform the school if at any time the conditions of the above program should change.

Student signature: _____

PARENT SECTION

I approve this request and release the school from responsibility for my child during times he/she is not assigned to class in the school. I understand that the school reserves the right to terminate the partial program arrangement if conditions change or if his/her academic program suffers.

Parent signature: _____

PROGRAM SUPERVISOR SECTION

This student is admitted to the program described above and will be supervised by me or by the person named below. I agree to inform the school if conditions of the program change before the end of the school year.

Phone: _____   Signature: _____

Address: _____

_____   Other personnel: _____

(Petition for Partial Senior Program, continued)

COUNSELOR SECTION

This student has currently earned a total of _____ credits toward graduation and will need _____ additional credits during grade 12 in order to graduate in June. I recommend that the administration take the following action in this case:

Periods affected: _____ Counselor signature: _____

ADMINISTRATOR SECTION

So long as the above conditions and approvals still obtain during the school year affected, I approve this request. This form is to be on file with the counselor until after graduation.

Date: _____ Administrator signature: _____

DEADLINE FOR RECEIPT OF THIS PETITION IN AN ADMINISTRATOR'S OFFICE IS JUNE 1.

This policy may be altered or petition disapproved without prior notice.

Application for Waiver of Course Requirements

Date: _____

To: Counselors

Re: Waivers of Course Requirements

The attached form is to be used for the student who does not meet the criteria to remain in a subject-area sequence, based on grades received in a prior course.

The form should be submitted before August 1 of the school year in which the waiver, if granted, would be in force.

The student and/or parent should supply a rationale in writing as to why the request for a waiver should be granted. Once the form has been completed, it should be submitted to the appropriate counselor for comment. The counselor should then send the form, along with the student's scholastic record, to the proper department supervisor.

Once the application for waiver has been approved or denied, the counselor should notify the family of the action taken, in case adjustments must be made to the student's schedule.

APPLICATION FOR WAIVER OF COURSE PREREQUISITES

STUDENT: _____

DATE OF REQUEST: _____

REQUEST TO TAKE: _____

IN PLACE OF: _____

Please attach a written statement listing the reason(s) why you are requesting this waiver. Note that we are asking for both student and parent/guardian signatures to the following.

The attached statement accurately expresses the circumstances and the reasons for the request.

Signatures:

Student _____ Parent/Guardian _____

FOR SCHOOL USE

Counselor Comments:

Subject-Area Supervisor:

                                        Approve: Yes   No   (circle one)
Comments:

Student/Parent-Initiated Course Change

Here is a form designed to shift course changes into low gear—one that gets more people involved in the change process and encourages a greater seriousness of purpose. Note that the parents have the opportunity to read staff comments and, therefore, are the last to sign.

■　　　■　　　■

STUDENT/PARENT-INITIATED COURSE CHANGE

Date: _____

I, _____, would like to drop _____
　　　　(Name of Student)　　　　　　　　　　　　　　　　(Course Title)

and add _____.
　　　　　　(Course or Study)

_____
(Student Signature)

Dear Drop Teacher:

Once appropriate signatures have been received, drop/add slips will be processed. The student is to remain in your class until the drop/add slips have been issued. The student *must* turn in the text to you prior to reporting to his or her new class. The counselor will help in this matter.

STEP 1.　I have met with the student and agree/disagree for the following reason(s):

_____

_____

WP　　WF
(Circle One)　　　　　　　　_____
　　　　　　　　　　　　　　　　　　(Teacher Signature)

DEPARTMENT CHAIR'S COMMENTS: _____

_____

_____
(Department Chair Signature)

(Student/Parent-Initiated Course Change, continued)

STEP 2.   I have met with my counselee and agree/disagree for the following reason(s):

_____

_____

_____

(Counselor Signature)

STEP 3.   I have read the above comments and discussed this change with my son/daughter. I believe it would/would not be in his/her best interest to make this change.

COMMENTS: _____

_____

_____

(Parent Signature)

Student/Parent-Initiated Course Change, variation

A variation on the same theme used by Watchung Hills Regional High School in Warren, New Jersey.

■　　■　　■

WATCHUNG HILLS REGIONAL HIGH SCHOOL
LATE APPLICATION FOR COURSE CHANGE

Student last name	first name	homeroom tchr	date	cslr	student code

Add course title	sem & period	days & room	teacher	ADD	course code

Drop course title	sem & period	days & room	teacher	DROP	course code

Per faculty policy, courses are NOT ADDED more than twenty-two school days after the term begins. STUDENT, PLEASE NOTE: This is only an *application;* YOU MUST ATTEND ALL ASSIGNED COURSES until the principal approves a change *after this form has been completed and reviewed.* EVERYONE, PLEASE NOTE: Complete sections below only in the order printed; include both a comment and your signature in all cases, approving or not. Thank you.

COMMENTS AND REASONS:　　　SIGNATURE & DATE:

STUDENT:

Parents must complete back before teachers are involved.

"DROP" TEACHER:
State size of class _____

"DROP" DEPT.
SUPERVISOR:

"ADD" TEACHER:
State size of class _____

"ADD" DEPT.
SUPERVISOR:

OTHER:

PRINCIPAL'S DECISION:

Reverse side, Student/Parent Initiated Course Change

To Parents:

Your youngster has asked to change a course that you approved at registration time last spring. Course selection at WHRHS is a carefully arranged series of steps progressing from February through July each year; it includes:

1. Recommendations by teachers and department chairpersons
2. Family study of the current program of studies
3. Preview programs orienting students to new courses
4. Preliminary selection of courses by students
5. Review of selections and recommendations by counselors
6. Reassessment based on spring and year-end progress reports
7. Notification of selections to parents, inviting reactions and changes
8. Preliminary scheduling "runs," with adjustments to avoid any period conflicts
9. Adjustments, as needed, to reflect any summer school work
10. Financial commitments to provide teachers and courses as chosen
11. Final programming by computer-scheduling procedures

Since course changes made *after* the year begins interfere with the educational progress of your youngster and the others in the classes affected, we are reluctant to upset schedules without careful examination of the *degree of need* for the change.

We ask you, therefore, to discuss very carefully with your youngster the need for a change *now*. Hopefully, ways can be found to "live with" the existing schedule this year, so that student and teacher programs are not upset at this late date. Perhaps the desired course can be taken next year or next semester (note that semester courses run for only ninety school days).

If the family still finds *strong, valid* reasons for changing now, we ask each parent to *comment* in writing below, indicating the *reasons:* (1) for the change and (2) for making the request at this time instead of during the previous registration period.

The final decision on such cases is the responsibility of the school principal. Please note that faculty policy precludes the addition of a new course later than twenty-two school days after the start of the term.

Father's comments and reasons:

_____

Father's signature and date

Mother's comments and reasons:

_____

Mother's signature and date

2. HOMEWORK AND STUDY HABITS

While the assignment and completion of homework/study is primarily the concern of the classroom teacher, the counselor can—and should—become involved in the handling *and prevention* of the consequences of failure to complete such activity properly. In conferences, counselors often hear parents lament the fact that their youngsters never bring any homework home. This in itself is certainly a significant problem worth exploring. An even more pervasive problem, however, is the misunderstanding students have as to what constitutes homework and what constitutes study. They love to lump the two together: When homework is done, so is study. As you know, the two terms are *not* synonymous.

You may also want to see Topic 7, *Behavior and Self-Esteem,* for a generic contract you can use to encourage homework and study routines.

Homework Recommendations for Parents

Dear Parent/Guardian:

Homework is one of the most powerful tools that can be used to ensure your child's success in school. As you know, the purpose of homework is to reinforce and extend what teachers have taught in the classroom.

Research indicates that students who consistently do their everyday homework: (a) improve academic achievement at all grade levels and (b) grow to be independent, responsible, motivated, and successful adults. Your involvement and support are vital in determining the motivation and success of your child.

You, as the parent, can help in the following ways:

1) Provide a study space where your child can work quietly with good lighting, room for materials, and freedom from distractions.
2) Consider with your child the amount of homework to be done, and plan a "time study schedule."
3) Be sure assignments are clearly written on your child's homework pad.
4) Offer positive reinforcement and encouragement. Emphasize the value of homework in helping your child practice skills and acquire information.
5) Grant your child "free time" when he/she has completed all homework assignments satisfactorily.
6) Periodically check your child's progress with his/her teacher.

Thank you for your concern. If you have any questions, please contact the Counseling Office.

Sincerely,

Counselor

Material/Supply List for Parents of Elementary Students

This kind of list has sometimes been used as part of a welcoming package sent by the elementary school in late summer.

■   ■   ■

MATERIAL/SUPPLY LIST

Dear Parent/Guardian:

It is very important that your child have all the necessary materials and supplies for school each day. Below is a sample supply list to help prepare your youngster for the school year.

———— pencil case

———— pens and pencils

———— erasers

———— homework/assignment pad

———— book covers

———— crayons and markers

———— three-ring binder/subject notebooks

———— lined notebook paper

———— subject dividers

———— other: ——————————————————————————

—————————————————————————————————————

—————————————————————————————————————

Please be sure your child's name is written on all items. Remember, you will have to replenish these items when necessary.

Thank you for your continued cooperation.

Sincerely yours,

————————————————————

Counselor

Homework Makeup Form

This form is used at the elementary and middle school levels to help youngsters gain skill in fulfilling their responsibilities.

■   ■   ■

HOMEWORK MAKEUP

Name: _____ Date: _____

Classwork assignments I missed:

Reading _____
_____
_____

Math _____
_____
_____

English/Language Arts _____
_____
_____

Spelling _____
_____
_____

Social Studies _____
_____
_____

Science _____
_____
_____

Other _____
_____
_____

Homework Makeup Form, variation

This form is employed by middle and/or junior high schools when a student has been absent for a minimum period of time, e.g., three days. The allowable "makeup period" is often set by the school, e.g., five days. The form can be obtained from the counselor and presented to teachers by the student.

■   ■   ■

HOMEWORK MAKEUP MEMO

STUDENT NAME: _____ UNIT: _____

DATE: _____

While you were absent from _____ to _____, you missed the following class assignments:

READING _____

_____

MATH _____

_____

ENGLISH _____

_____

SOCIAL STUDIES _____

_____

SCIENCE _____

_____

OTHER _____

_____

_____

Please complete the above assignments and submit them to your teachers by

_____.

_____
Counselor

Homework Notice

If a student continually comes to school without his/her homework—or fails to even take the assignments home—perhaps it's time to start a formal homework procedure.

■   ■   ■

HOMEWORK NOTICE

Date: _____

Dear _____,

We consider homework to be an important part of your child's education. _____ _____, however, has not handed in several assignments. Some of the dates on which homework was missing are:

_____

_____

Homework is a factor in providing lifelong skills as well as in determining the amount of knowledge gained and the grade received in a subject. We urge your assistance in correcting this situation.

Sincerely,

_____

Counselor

. . . . Please detach and return to school . . . .

Student's name: _____   Class: _____

I have read the homework notice dated: _____

I would like to come in to talk about this on: _____

or

I would appreciate your telephoning me.

Parent's comments: _____

_____

_____

_____

_____

Parent/Guardian signature

Notice to Parents of Homework Contract

STUDENT RESPONSIBILITIES

Dear Parent/Guardian:

For your child's sake, homework needs to be a priority in your household. He/she must have an appropriate place in which to work and a definite time in his/her schedule to complete assignments. You should supervise "Homework Time" in your home.

Since your youngster has not been fulfilling his/her responsibility to complete homework assignments, it is time to institute a formal homework contract.

Your son/daughter should:

1. Write all homework assignments in a memo pad.
2. Bring home all necessary materials, such as books, workbooks, dittos, etc.
3. File his/her homework in a notebook section or in a special place, so that he/she will be able to find it easily for class the next day.
4. Provide a section of his/her notebook for tests and quizzes, so that you will be able to review them.

You will need to check completed homework at the end of the homework session each day.

Thank you for your cooperation.

                                            Sincerely yours,

                                            _____
                                            Counselor

Notices to Teachers of Homework Contract

When a formal homework contract has been arranged, the following notices can be sent to each of the student's teachers; the first is for the start of the program, the second for its conclusion.

■   ■   ■

Date: _____

Counselor: _____

To: _____

For your information:

I have initiated the Formal Assignment Pad Process with _____

_____. The process will begin on _____
and last for four weeks. If, during this period, this student does not comply with the process, please notify me. I will be seeing the student once each week.

Thank you!

· ·

Date: _____

Counselor: _____

To: _____

For your information:

I have seen _____ for the last time about the
Formal Assignment Pad Process. If, within the next week, you see a decrease in the homework assignments being handed in, please notify me immediately so that I can follow up and reinitiate the Formal Assignment Pad Process.

Thank you!

Homework Monitoring Sheet

ASSIGNMENTS: WEEKLY REPORT

NAME: _____ DATE: _____

TEACHER: _____

Teacher, please mark and initial: + = completed daily assignment
0 = incomplete assignment

MONDAY	TUESDAY	WEDNESDAY	THURSDAY	FRIDAY

Parent/Guardian Signature

Please return to counselor!

Daily Homework Worksheet

The following chart is designed to help a student record all of his/her assignments. If no homework is assigned, a student writes "no homework," which is initialed by the teacher for verification.

■   ■   ■

DAILY HOMEWORK WORKSHEET

If there is no homework, write "no homework" and have the teacher initial it.

| Day: _____ | | Day: _____ | |
| Date: _____ | | Date: _____ | |
Subject	Homework	Subject	Homework

| Day: _____ | | Day: _____ | |
| Date: _____ | | Date: _____ | |
Subject	Homework	Subject	Homework

| Day: _____ | |
| Date: _____ | |
Subject	Homework

PARENT'S SIGNATURE:

_____

COUNSELOR'S SIGNATURE:

_____

COMMENTS: _____

_____

_____

_____

Elementary School Homework Log

ELEMENTARY SCHOOL HOMEWORK LOG

NAME: _____ DATE: _____

SUBJECT	HOMEWORK ASSIGNMENT	TEACHER'S INITIALS
Reading		
Math		
Language Arts		
Spelling		
Social Studies		
Science		
Other		

Homework Pad Instructions

IMPORTANT STEPS FOR RECORDING ASSIGNMENTS

In your homework pad:

- Write the date(s) at the top of the page(s).
- Write down every assignment.
- Check off an assignment after you have completed it.
- Record test dates in *color*.
- Write "Test Study" when you should prepare for tests.

Long-term assignments should be broken down into several steps. For example: To write a report you will have to decide on a topic, do research, outline your thoughts, write a rough draft, edit the draft, and write the final copy. Use a weekly calendar to record the beginning of each step.

You can use the form below to record specific steps for long-term assignments.

LONG-TERM ASSIGNMENTS

The assignment

is _____

_____

_____

Date of assignment: _____   Date due: _____

Steps: Starting date:

1. _____   _____

2. _____   _____

3. _____   _____

4. _____   _____

5. _____   _____

6. _____   _____

Daily Homework Schedule

This form can be used by students having difficulty completing assignments in an appropriate amount of time. Students should learn to budget their "afterschool" time, just as their school hours are scheduled.

■   ■   ■

DAILY HOMEWORK SCHEDULE

MONDAY/Homework Time

3:00 P.M.	7:00 P.M.
3:30 P.M.	7:30 P.M.
4:00 P.M.	8:00 P.M.
4:30 P.M.	8:30 P.M.
5:00 P.M.	9:00 P.M.
5:30 P.M.	9:30 P.M.
6:00 P.M.	10:00 P.M.
6:30 P.M.	10:30 P.M.

TUESDAY/Homework Time

3:00 P.M.	7:00 P.M.
3:30 P.M.	7:30 P.M.
4:00 P.M.	8:00 P.M.
4:30 P.M.	8:30 P.M.
5:00 P.M.	9:00 P.M.
5:30 P.M.	9:30 P.M.
6:00 P.M.	10:00 P.M.
6:30 P.M.	10:30 P.M.

WEDNESDAY/Homework Time

3:00 P.M.	7:00 P.M.
3:30 P.M.	7:30 P.M.
4:00 P.M.	8:00 P.M.
4:30 P.M.	8:30 P.M.
5:00 P.M.	9:00 P.M.
5:30 P.M.	9:30 P.M.
6:00 P.M.	10:00 P.M.
6:30 P.M.	10:30 P.M.

(Daily Homework Schedule, continued)

THURSDAY/Homework Time

3:00 P.M.	7:00 P.M.
3:30 P.M.	7:30 P.M.
4:00 P.M.	8:00 P.M.
4:30 P.M.	8:30 P.M.
5:00 P.M.	9:00 P.M.
5:30 P.M.	9:30 P.M.
6:00 P.M.	10:00 P.M.
6:30 P.M.	10:30 P.M.

FRIDAY/Homework Time

3:00 P.M.	7:00 P.M.
3:30 P.M.	7:30 P.M.
4:00 P.M.	8:00 P.M.
4:30 P.M.	8:30 P.M.
5:00 P.M.	9:00 P.M.
5:30 P.M.	9:30 P.M.
6:00 P.M.	10:00 P.M.
6:30 P.M.	10:30 P.M.

Homework Hints for Parents

Dear Parent/Guardian:

In conferences with parents we frequently hear, "There is no homework." The point needs to be made that although no specific homework has been assigned, there *is* still homework: It's called study time. We strongly recommend that all students spend a *minimum* of one half hour of homework/study time (five days a week) on each academic subject pursued. If your son or daughter has no studying to do, in order to fill this 2½ hour time frame he/she should read a good book.

Working together, we need to stress to our young people that study, in contrast to specified homework, includes (but is not limited to):

1. Rewriting classroom lecture notes or lab reports
2. Checking lecture notes while they are still fresh in a student's mind; in terms of understanding material, one hour spent as soon after a lecture as possible is worth several hours a few days later
3. Outlining an English or science chapter to use to review for a quiz or chapter test
4. Rethinking, e.g., using foreign language vocabulary words by making up sentences and transcribing them in the foreign language
5. Reviewing, e.g., reviewing theorems in geometry so one knows them verbatim and can apply them to problems not previously assigned
6. Getting a good night's sleep before a test—no cramming! Research indicates that sleep aids in "sealing in" information
7. If there isn't any studying to do—READ!!!

Sincerely,

_____

Counselor

Communication Tips: Dealing with Low Grades

COMMUNICATION TIPS FOR EVERYONE

WHEN A LOW GRADE SHOWS UP . . . on an Interim Warning notice or a Progress Report, parents or teachers can become anxious about the problem and resort to blaming, scolding, or "grounding"—which may not result in improvement.

It might be more effective to have a discussion in which the adults recognize the youngster's own disappointment and where together they work out a plan of action for improvement. (It is important to remember that it is the *student's* responsibility to take the lead in diagnosing the problem, suggesting solutions, and working the situation through.)

Here are some questions worth discussing with the youngster—and some brief reasons for asking each:

"What seems to be the problem as *you* see it?"
(The answer may surprise you. It could be an excuse or the truth.)

"Why are you taking this course?"
(Requirement for graduation? For college? For a job? Let *him/her* say it!)

"Do you plan to take the next course in this area next year?"
(Most sequential courses depend on success in the previous course; the course may already be scheduled.)

"What steps have you *already* taken to improve the situation?"
(If answers sound like "put-ons," note that most youngsters are slow to take action.)

"How is the rest of school going at this point?"
(A chance to relax by discussing happier situations.)

"Are you involved in any activities?" (or, "How are your activities going?")
(Some school involvement generally means better grades!)

"Does the way you spend time after school affect this problem in any way?"
(Some relaxation is needed, but "goofing off" instead of homework . . .)

(Communication Tips, continued)

"What do YOU think might be some good courses of action?"
(The burden of coming up with solutions should be shouldered in part by the youngster.)

"What are the good points and bad points of your plans for action?"
(Some cures are worse than the disease!)

"What can we agree are the *best* steps to take *now* to attack the problem?"
(The steps should be mutually acceptable to all concerned and must represent a *firm* program of *change.*)

"How soon (number of days!) should I call the teacher/parent to see if your plan of action is in fact correcting the situation?"
(Follow-through on the agreements is the whole point; improvement must be *made,* not just talked about!)

When a student's own attempts to correct a course problem have not produced the hoped-for results, the teacher and parent should be in direct contact in order to explore other avenues.

Letter to Students: Improving Vocabulary

PAINLESS WAYS TO INCREASE YOUR VOCABULARY

Dear Student:

During July and August you are bound to dream of sun, surf, and sand. But remember: The summer is also the perfect season to set aside some time for reading.

Students and parents often wonder how comprehension and vocabulary—and, consequently, SAT scores—can be improved. The answer is simple. Read! Read! Read!

Consider devoting at least one half hour every day to reading newspapers (preferably *The New York Times*) and such weekly magazines as *Time* and *Newsweek* in order to improve reading skills and keep informed about current events. Some time should also be set aside for the pleasurable reading of magazines and books that reflect your individual interests.

Crossword puzzles, word searches, cryptoquotes, and games like Scrabble are always fun ways to improve one's vocabulary.

Or, you might want to practice taking all or part of an SAT under simulated conditions. Find a quiet, undisturbed area, set a timer, and take the test. Be sure to correct it, noting errors and checking for unfamiliar vocabulary.

Remember the old adage: "Practice makes perfect." And, there is no better way to enhance your vocabulary and reading skills than by studying under relaxed conditions. So go to it!

Sincerely,

_____

Counseling Department

Letter to Parents: When Your Child Says "I'm Bored"

THE "B" WORD

Dear Parent/Guardian:

When you first hear your child state, "I'm bored," you may be thrown off guard. Let's face it, everyone gets bored from time to time. But, we don't expect young children to become bored, yet they do—or at least they say that they do.

What issues are behind a child's use of the "B" word?

1. It can be used as an attention-getting mechanism. Saying "I'm bored" is a sure way of getting parental attention. Suggesting things to do to the child can bring a continual response of "no," "no way," or "forget it." Ask yourself a question: Is your child genuinely unable to go along with a suggested activity, or has he gained what he really wanted—a half hour or so of your undivided attention?

2. Your child's peers may be encouraging him to act bored because it's an "in thing" with a particular group. This kind of attitude usually passes rather quickly. Your best response is to "roll" with it; be tolerant and keep your sense of humor.

3. Some children who act bored just don't feel like doing the work. They may even send a message indicating that a difficult task can be accomplished, but they don't want to be bothered doing it. Here you might want to encourage your child to acknowledge and *understand* that success does not always come easily; that buckling down to hard work, whether one feels like it or not, can pay big dividends.

4. Schoolwork that is "too easy" can produce boredom. Schools try to challenge every student every day. On occasion a student will grasp a concept or a set of skills well before her classmates. She may have to learn to exercise patience while classmates catch up. On the other hand, if such periodic boredom becomes more the norm than the exception, you may want to check to ensure that your child's educational placement level is a proper one.

5. A child may become "bored" if the work is indeed too difficult; it is easier to claim boredom than to admit defeat. Check with the child's teacher to make sure that he/she is able to do the task and/or does not have an undiagnosed learning disability.

6. Children who are overstructured are often lost when faced with "nothing to do." "I'm bored" may simply mean that your child does not know how to handle free time appropriately. It is important that children learn that life is not a totally organized experience. Having "nothing to do" can open the door to doing some really neat things. Just ask any adult!

Sincerely,

_____

Counseling Department

Peer Tutoring Information for Parents

A formal peer tutoring program requires a fair amount of paperwork, but the professional attitude it imparts often yields professional results.

■   ■   ■

_____

Date

Dear Parent/Guardian:

In order to provide all students with the opportunity to obtain good quality extra help in weak subject areas, our school has instituted a "Peer Tutoring Club." Qualified volunteer students have been trained to be tutors in a variety of subjects by _____ _____, the club advisor.

The Peer Tutoring Club will meet daily, Monday through Thursday, after school in room(s) _____ from _____ P.M. to _____ P.M. Students who remain after school for peer tutoring sessions will be provided transportation home by the "late" buses.

You should encourage your child to attend at least one peer tutoring session in order to experience students helping each other. If you feel strongly that your youngster could benefit from this program—or if his/her teacher recommends participation—you might consider requiring your youngster to attend on a given day each week or when help is needed.

If you have any questions regarding the Peer Tutoring Club, please contact the club advisor or the Counseling Office.

Thank you for your continued support.

Sincerely yours,

_____

Director of Counseling

Recommendation Form for Potential Peer Tutors

RECOMMENDATION FORM FOR POTENTIAL PEER TUTORS

_____
(Date)

To: _____
    (Advisor of Peer Tutoring Club)

I am recommending _____

    Grade: _____ Homeroom number: _____

to be a tutor in the Peer Tutoring Club.

Subject area(s) of strength are: _____

_____

Comments concerning potential peer tutor: _____

_____

_____

_____

_____
(Referring Teacher/Counselor)

Peer Tutoring Referral

REFERRAL FORM TO RECOMMEND TUTORING FOR A STUDENT

_____

(Date)

Peer Tutoring Club Advisor:

Student recommended for tutoring by Peer Tutoring Club:

_____

Grade: _____ Homeroom number: _____

Subject(s) in which tutoring is needed: _____

_____

Specific areas in textbook(s) that need to be covered:

_____

_____

_____

(Counselor/Teacher)

. . . .

Potential Tutoring Assignment

(To be completed by club advisor)

_____

(Date)

Student tutor: _____

Grade: _____ Homeroom: _____

Comments: _____

_____

_____

_____

(Advisor)

Peer Tutoring Recommendation to Parents

RECOMMENDATION FOR TUTORING TO PARENT/GUARDIAN

Date: _____

To: Parent/Guardian of _____

Re: Peer Tutoring Club

Dear _____:

It has been suggested by his/her teacher that _____ could benefit greatly in his/her study of _____ by being helped by the Peer Tutoring Club. Young people are often of great assistance to each other.

If I don't hear from you to the contrary, we will set up a session for _____ and a peer tutor.

Please contact me or the counselor if you have any questions.

Thank you for your support.

_____
Club Advisor

Peer Tutor Assignment/Report

PEER TUTOR ASSIGNMENT

Date: _____

To: Student tutor: _____

    Grade: _____ Homeroom: _____

Re: Student: _____

    Grade: _____ Homeroom: _____

Subject: _____

Areas to be covered: _____

_____

_____

. . . .

Upon Completion:

Date: _____

To: Advisor: _____

From: Student tutor: _____

    Grade: _____ Homeroom: _____

Re: Student: _____

    Grade: _____ Homeroom: _____

Subject: _____

Areas covered: _____

_____

_____

_____
(Tutor's signature)

3. PROGRESS REPORTS AND WARNINGS

Although the next two reports are sent by teachers, counselors have to deal with the findings. Counselors might want to have input into the design of such forms.

Academic Progress Report

ACADEMIC PROGRESS REPORT

STUDENT NAME: _____ GRADE: _____

SUBJECT: _____ DATE: _____ QUARTER: _____

The purpose of this interim report is to inform you of your son/daughter's current performance in the above-mentioned course.

General Status:

_____ Earned letter grade of D or F

_____ Dropped more than one letter grade since the last marking period

_____ Shows significant improvement since the last marking period

Improvement is needed in the following area(s):

_____ Class Attendance

_____ Class Assignments/Preparation

_____ Class Participation/Cooperation

_____ Homework/Study

_____ Test Scores

Recommendation(s) include:

_____ More serious approach to study

_____ Increased effort and time in preparation for class

_____ Taking advantage of afterschool assistance

_____ Tutorial assistance

_____ Parent/teacher conference

Additional Comments: _____

_____

Thank you for your continued cooperation and support.

_____
                                                            Teacher

Copies: White—Parent   Yellow—Counselor   Pink—Teacher

Notice of Unsatisfactory Work

GUIDANCE DEPARTMENT
FISHER JUNIOR HIGH SCHOOL
LOWER FERRY ROAD
TRENTON, NJ

INTERIM REPORT

Date: _____

To the Parent or Guardian of:

_____ Homeroom _____ Grade 7, 8, 9

Subject: _____ Teacher: _____

Dear Parent or Guardian:

_____ is doing unsatisfactory work in

_____, possibly because of the following reason(s):

[ ] Class discussion   [ ] Behavior problem   [ ] Daily effort
[ ] Wastes time   [ ] Inattentive   [ ] Test scores
[ ] Class work incomplete   [ ] Does not seek extra help [ ] Absent too often
[ ] Homework incomplete   [ ] Poor understanding   [ ] Comes unprepared
[ ] Carelessness   [ ] Lack of basic skills   [ ] Poor attitude
[ ] Project incomplete

Additional comments:

If you wish to discuss this matter, please feel free to telephone me between _____

and _____ daily.

Very truly yours,

_____
Teacher

PUPIL—White copy; TEACHER—Yellow copy; COUNSELOR—Pink copy

Addressing Failing Grades

The dictionary defines a loser as "one who consistently fails." Many of the students labeled "losers" have certainly been consistent: They've been working at losing for years, sometimes through no fault of their own. Some people feel that losers have been born to fail. Others believe that societal factors (child neglect/abuse, messy divorce situations, poverty, substance abuse by youngster or parent, lower ability level than peers) may have kept a youngster down so far that he can't get up by himself. No matter whether this is or is not true, the counselor's formidable challenge is to turn losers into winners *now*.

We hope the entries included here will assist you in turning your failing students into achievers.

■   ■   ■

Failure Warning to Parents

May 1, _____

Dear Parent(s):

In accordance with the provisions of the Stratford Township Board of Education Policy #639, we are informing you that your child, _____, is in serious danger of failing the course(s) listed below, which may affect promotion to the next grade level.

Time is still available for your child to raise his or her grades, but your *immediate* attention is required.

Please contact your child's counselor right away, in order to develop an appropriate plan of action.

Sincerely,

_____
Thomas R. Lewis
Principal

Name of Counselor: _____

Failing Courses: _____

_____

_____

Request for Conference with Parent

WATCHUNG HILLS REGIONAL HIGH SCHOOL   PHONE: 647-1511
Warren, New Jersey 07059

Date: _____

Re: _____

Dear Parent:

Your youngster (named above) has been experiencing difficulty in one or more courses required for promotion or graduation. Incomplete or failing grades for three marking periods normally result in the loss of credit for the year's work in that particular course.

Our experience indicates, however, that a drastic change in habits of attendance and performance can be successful in correcting the kind of problems that lead to failure.

Please telephone the high school today (at the number given above) in order to arrange for an appointment with the teacher(s) involved and/or with me, so that we can review the seriousness of this situation and set up a definite program for change. The student should also be present at this meeting.

We share your concern for the success of your youngster, and we look forward to hearing from you as soon as possible. We don't have time to waste.

Yours truly,

_____
Counselor

Teacher Report: Students in Danger of Retention

This is a possible retention list from classroom teachers to the Counseling Department.

■   ■   ■

Teacher: _____

Subject: _____

Date: _____

To: All Teaching Staff

From: The Counseling Department

Re: Possible Retentions

Please list the name of each student who is in danger of failing your class for the year. Since the Counseling Department will be compiling this information prior to the issuance of third quarter report cards, please provide first, second, and third quarter grades.

We need to have your completed form by _____.
                                                                    (Date)
Letters will be sent to the parent(s) of every student in danger of being retained.

Thank you for your cooperation.

                                                        _____
                                                                    (Counselor)

Student	*Class*	*1st Qtr.*	*2nd Qtr.*	*3rd Qtr.*
_____	_____	_____	_____	_____
_____	_____	_____	_____	_____
_____	_____	_____	_____	_____
_____	_____	_____	_____	_____

Retention Warning to Parents

_____
(Date)

Dear Parent/Guardian:

During the first three marking periods, we sent you various pieces of information regarding your child's academic progress: progress reports, parent conference notices, and report cards. After reviewing our records, it has been determined that _____ may fail the following subject(s):

_____

_____

If your child fails these subjects in the last quarter, he/she could be retained for the following year.

We suggest that you work closely with your child, so that his/her fourth quarter grades sufficiently raise his/her average to a passing level.

We will continue to monitor your child's progress and, of course, notify you if summer school is recommended or required.

Sincerely yours,

_____
Anne Melnick
Counselor

Referral to Student Assistance Program (SAP)

In some school districts, students who are failing two or more subjects, and/or are not completing class and homework assignments, or whose work has shown a marked decrease in quality are referred to a Student Assistant Specialist. Any professional staff member can make a referral.

■   ■   ■

SAP REFERRAL FORM

Date: _____

Student's name: _____   Number: _____

Grade: _____

Counselor: _____

Referring person: _____   Subject: _____

Reason for referral: _____

Please check relevant items:

I. Academic Performance
_____ Current grade average _____
_____ Incomplete assignments
_____ Decline in quality of work
_____ Underachieving

II. Classroom Conduct
_____ Disruptive in class
_____ Lack of concentration
_____ Works below potential
_____ Inattentive during class

III. Physical
_____ Drowsiness
_____ Frequent complaints of illness
_____ Personal appearance
_____ Poor coordination
_____ Bruises/unexplained injuries
_____ Other _____

IV. Behavior
_____ Hyperactivity
_____ Withdrawn, very quiet
_____ Defiance of rules
_____ Obscene behavior
_____ Death themes
_____ Personality changes

V. Attendance
_____ Frequent absences
_____ Often late to class/school
_____ Frequent cutting of class
_____ Other _____

VI. Other Behavior
_____ Change in friends
_____ Unexplained popularity
_____ Seeks adult attention
_____ Compulsive overachievement

List actions already taken: _____

_____

_____

_____

Signature

Summer School Recommendation

_____
(Date)

Dear Parent/Guardian:

It has been recommended by his/her teacher(s) that your child, _____,
would benefit by taking the following course(s) in summer school:

_____

_____

Enclosed is a registration form for your completion. Please return it to the Counseling
Office by _____.
                (Date)

Although summer school enrollment is not mandatory for promotion to the next
grade, we believe it would be educationally beneficial for your child to attend summer
school.

If you have any further questions, don't hesitate to telephone us here at the Counseling
Office.

Sincerely yours,

_____
Barry Iscovitz
Counselor

Endangered Graduation Warning to Parents

A warning letter is sent at midyear and again at the end of the third quarter to the parents of "endangered" seniors. Note the personal manner in which the counselor is tied to the family. Note also that the student in question is mentioned *first* among the participants in the action.

■   ■   ■

Date: _____

Dear _____ :
     (parent/guardian)

A review of _____'s midyear grades indicates that he/she may not be able to graduate in June for the following reason(s):

I am alerting you *now* so that _____, you, and I can take the necessary action to make it possible for him/her to graduate with the class. It would be most beneficial if you telephoned me here at the high school or made an appointment to see me in person to discuss this matter. I would like to be as helpful as possible at this point in time.

I look forward to hearing from you.

Sincerely,

_____
Counselor

Retention Warning to Parents of Juniors

This type of letter does not mean that the final curtain is completely down; after all, "Where there's a will, there's a way." Students have even been known to skip lunch in order to graduate with their class. Nonetheless, schools find it particularly important to face the issue directly by retaining at the end of the eleventh year and officially notifying parents of such retention. Here is where close communication between home and counselor is imperative.

■   ■   ■

Date: _____

Dear Parent/Guardian:

A review of _____'s records indicates that he or she has not earned the required number (90) of credits to be considered a senior and, therefore, is being retained in grade 11.

Diplomas are awarded to those students who have successfully completed 120 credits in grades 9 through 12. Under the present circumstances, your youngster may not be able to graduate with his/her class. It is therefore critical that you contact his/her counselor to discuss this matter.

Yours truly,

_____
George R. Benson
Principal

4. EXCEPTIONAL STUDENTS

The letters and forms in this section will help you meet the needs of many special populations: students who need extra help in basic skills, students requiring English as a Second Language instruction, students participating in a gifted and talented program, and students who receive special services as part of their individual educational program (IEP).

Counselors have always dealt with the gifted and talented, but many have been hesitant to deal with the handicapped; some welcome the opportunity to serve, while others continue to see themselves as inadequate to the task, probably due to a lack of formal training. This is one reason for a close working relationship between school counselors and sensitive child study team (CST) members, who can be most helpful to reluctant counselors in helping to close any training gap. Counselors can then work with special services to plan a counselee's yearly schedule, help develop an individual educational program, and consult with parents both privately and on a case-conference basis.

If you decide to do a bit of in-house retraining, a sensible first step is for you and special services to analyze staff needs jointly. Planners might want workshop content to focus heavily on counseling methodology. Individual counseling techniques, such as behavior modification, client-centered therapy, and reality therapy, appear to be especially useful in counseling the disabled. Role playing and values clarification have been found to be beneficial group counseling techniques.

Disabled youngsters themselves have always had the same wide-ranging needs as their nonexceptional counterparts. And, thanks to the 1975 federally sponsored Education for All Handicapped Children Act, these needs are being more fully addressed in an effort to maximize educational, social, physical, and vocational potential.

Gifted and Talented Students

Gifted and talented youngsters have their own special problems. And, like the educationally handicapped, they often suffer from an impaired self-image, caused in part by years of extreme anxiety and unrelenting pressure to excel academically.

Some educators believe that these young people are so self-directed that they don't need the same attention as typical students: "They're bright and talented—they'll pull it off." Nothing could be further from the truth! A talented and gifted child needs a counselor as much as the next person—maybe even more. And so do their parents.

Yes, being gifted and talented isn't easy. Then again, being exceptional in *any* way isn't easy.

■   ■   ■

Myths About the Gifted and Talented

This can be distributed to faculty and/or used as the basis for a seminar.

■　　■　　■

COMMON MYTHS ABOUT G & Ts

- Gifted students are a homogeneous group; they are all high achievers.
- Gifted students do not need help: If they are really gifted, they can manage on their own.
- Gifted students have fewer problems than others, because their intelligence and abilities somehow exempt them from the hassles of daily life.
- The future of the gifted student is assured: A world of opportunities lies before the student.
- Gifted students are self-directed: They know where they are headed.
- The social and emotional development of the gifted student is at the same level as his or her intellectual development.
- Gifted students just need to be pushed to try harder; they need to get organized.
- Gifted students are social isolates.
- The primary value of the gifted student lies in his or her brainpower.
- The gifted student's family always prizes his or her abilities.
- Gifted students need to serve as examples to others and should always assume extra responsibility.
- Gifted students can accomplish anything they put their minds to, all they have to do is apply themselves.

Individual Basic Skills Placement Form

This is completed by teachers as students move from an elementary to a middle school setting.

■   ■   ■

INDIVIDUAL BASIC SKILLS PLACEMENT FORM

STUDENT: _____   BUILDING: _____

GRADE LEVEL: _____

RECOMMENDING TEACHER: _____

Please circle the appropriate area(s):

Reading   Math   Writing

CRITERIA:

1. The student's minimum levels of proficiency (MLP) are as follows:

   Total National Percentiles   Reading _____

                                       Math   _____

                                       Writing _____

2. The projected final report card grade is _____.

Notice of Recommendation for Basic Skills Improvement Program

CRESTWOOD ELEMENTARY SCHOOL
SMART BOULEVARD
POPLAR BLUFF, MD 63901

Basic Skills Improvement Program

_____
Date

To the Parent/Guardian of _____:

Because all of our children have different strengths and weaknesses, Crestwood Elementary School provides special academic assistance to certain qualified children through the Basic Skills Improvement Program (BSIP).

Your child, _____, has been identified and recommended to receive assistance through BSIP in the following areas:

To be eligible for participation, a child must be recommended by a teacher and obtain specific scores on the most recent standardized tests. Instruction is administered during the regular school session by trained specialists in mathematics, reading, and/or writing.

If you have any questions or concerns about the program, please contact the Counseling Office. We will be happy to talk with you.

Sincerely yours,

_____
Deborah Laird
Counselor

Parent Notification of ESL Program Participation

English as a Second Language is part of the course-selection process. Where there is no ESL director, counselors are often responsible for contacting the home. At the very least, they should be aware of the communication. Since parents may not read English, you should try to get appropriate translations of ESL program notifications.

■   ■   ■

HILLTOP MIDDLE SCHOOL
300 LONG ROAD
MANFORD, OK 74044

Parent/Guardian

Address

City/State/Zip

_____
                                                          (Date)

Dear Parent/Guardian:

I would like to inform you that your son/daughter, _____, has been selected to participate in the school district's "English as a Second Language (ESL)" program.

_____ will be instructed in the skills of listening, speaking, reading, and writing in the English language.

It is our hope that he/she will become better acquainted with spoken and written English.

If you have any questions regarding this program, don't hesitate to contact me here at the Counseling Office. I can be reached at _____.

Sincerely,

_____
Counselor

Parent Notification of ESL Program Participation (Spanish Version)

Here is a direct translation of the previous parent notification. If no one in the Counseling Office speaks Spanish, you may need to have the last paragraph changed so as to direct parents to someone who can converse with them.

■   ■   ■

HILLTOP MIDDLE SCHOOL
300 LONG ROAD
MANFORD, OK 74044

Parent/Guardian

Address

City/State/Zip

_____

(Date)

Querido padre/madre/guardián:

Quiero informarle que su hijo(a), _____, ha sido seleccionado(a) como un(a) participante del programa, "Inglés como un Segundo Idioma," de nuestro distrito escolar.

_____ será intruído en las destrezas de escuchar, conversar, leer y escribir en el idioma inglés.

Es nuestro deseo que el/ella se familiarice con el inglés hablado y escrito.

Si Ud. tiene alguna pregunta con relación a este programa, favor de contactarme en la Oficina de Consejería. Puede localizarme llamando al teléfono _____.

Atentamente,

_____

Consejero

Student Evaluation Request

This is a referral form from the counselor to the teacher requesting information for the child study team; it is appropriate for the elementary level.

■   ■   ■

STUDENT EVALUATION REQUEST

To: _____   Date: _____

Re: _____   Grade: _____

Would you please give me a thumbnail sketch of _____,
using the space below? Include comments concerning the child's social, emotional, and academic achievement or difficulty; attitude and effort; suspected physical or emotional difficulties; unusual behavior; or any other information you consider to be significant. This information will be maintained as CONFIDENTIAL; however, it will be included in our referral to the school psychologist.

Thank you for your assistance!

_____
Counselor

_____
Teacher

Educationally Handicapped Students

Specifications about a disabled student's schedule for the ensuing year can be sent from the child study team to the counselor by memo, but this obviously minimizes intercommunication. For other handicapped students, scheduling is conducted in conjunction with a regular IEP meeting, with parents and student present. A third approach is to hold special annual prescheduling conferences, where the team, special education teachers, and counselor can work out the best possible schedule for each student; the counselor then has a private session with the youngster. Whatever the approach you use, if you want to make a difference, go prepared.

■   ■   ■

Staff Memo: Scheduling Handicapped Students

DATE: _____

TO: ALL COUNSELORS

FROM: FRANK HENRY, DIRECTOR OF COUNSELING

RE: SCHEDULING OF HANDICAPPED STUDENTS

On February 24, the special services team and all special education teachers will meet with counselors in the team conference room to assist in the scheduling of our handicapped students. Counselors should bring the following items to this meeting:

1. A copy of each student's transcript
2. A copy of the most recent report card
3. A copy of his/her current schedule
4. Any anecdotal records appropriate for making an informed decision about next year's schedule

Attached is a copy of scheduled meeting times.

Thank you!

Suspension Review of Handicapped Students

In New Jersey, as in certain other states, a child study team must review the status of an educationally handicapped student who is suspended from school. The CST must also set forth in writing its conclusions and recommendations, if any, regarding the questions listed below.

■   ■   ■

SUSPENSION REVIEW FORM

Today's Date: _____

Student's Name: _____

Date of Incident: _____

Date(s) of Suspension: _____

Type of Suspension: ( ) In-School   ( ) Out-of-School

Administrator: _____

No   Yes   Was the behavior that resulted in suspension primarily caused by
( )   ( )   the student's handicapped condition?

If yes, please explain:

No   Yes   Is the student's individualized educational program appropriate at
( )   ( )   this time?

If no, please explain:

Last IEP update: _____

Child Study Team Recommendations:

cc: Parent(s)
    Principal/Assistant Principal
    CST Case Manager
    Counselor

Special Education Placement Recommendations

This particular placement form is completed by the child study team (CST) and by classroom teachers. Middle school counselors utilize the recommendations to place their counselees in appropriate courses.

■   ■   ■

EAST BRUNSWICK PUBLIC SCHOOLS
HAMMARSKJOLD MIDDLE SCHOOL
GUIDANCE DEPARTMENT

SPECIAL EDUCATION PLACEMENT RECOMMENDATIONS

STUDENT NAME: _____ GRADE: _____

CASE MANAGER: _____

TEACHERS: _____

_____

_____

_____

Self-Contained Class (Please indicate most appropriate class.)

Good Skills/Good Work Habits	Advanced _____
Average Skills/Erratic Work Habits	Developmental _____
Poor Skills/Poor Work Habits	Remedial _____
Very Poor Skills/Makes Effort	Basic _____

Resource Room Replacement (Please indicate appropriate placements.)

Resource Room Reading	_____
Resource Room English	_____
Resource Room Math	_____
Resource Room Study Skills	_____

Mainstream Placements (Please circle appropriate ability level.)

Reading:	Advanced	Developmental	Remedial	Basic Skills
English:	Advanced	Developmental	Remedial	Basic Skills
Math:	Advanced	Developmental	Remedial	Basic Skills

Special Considerations/Comments Regarding Mainstream Placements:

_____

_____

_____

5.   TESTING AND CURRICULUM

Standardized testing programs continue to occupy an integral place in our schools because staff personnel continue to see definite benefits to them, even if certain critics do not.

Test results *do* influence curriculum development. Since counselors have a role in such development as suggesters for the addition, modification, or elimination of certain courses, they should be involved in any testing program. The question is, "How?"

There are those who believe that the *administration* of standardized tests is not a legitimate counseling function. But even those who say "no" to test administration, usually say "yes" to test interpretation. These professionals agree that the counselors' valuable role in advising students on course selection, which in itself draws upon test results, demands that counselors play a significant role in the school's entire testing program.

Of course, we need to place a high priority on the thorough and comprehensive communication of test results. Machines will never replace the human touch, with its potential for positive reinforcement. You can help your counselee find real meaning in test results by: (1) supporting and encouraging continued achievement; (2) reaching out with a multitude of suggestions as to what can be done with newly acquired self-knowledge; and (3) assisting in sorting through feelings as career and postsecondary school options are explored.

School counselors can influence the shaping of curriculum at all educational levels. If the definition of the term "curriculum" is broadened to include so-called *extra*curricular activities, counselors can make an even greater impact on curriculum development. Curriculum in its broadest sense includes *all* the planned learning experiences that a school can offer.

Counselors should be seen by students and other staff personnel as fellow educators with important knowledge to share. Many began their educational careers in a classroom; returning to that scene occasionally can be an enlightening, rewarding, and broadening experience. Counselors can develop a greater feel for the school's personality and focus.

We should "step into" the school curriculum from time to time and actually teach counseling-related topics to students. A broad-based, developmental college admission program will put us squarely there, for instance. There is plenty of appropriate material for us to teach—self-assessment, stress management, understanding sexuality, the handling of crises, substance abuse prevention, the development of real independence—to name only a few potential programs.

For student and parent information about college admissions testing, such as the SAT and ACH, see Topic 12, *College Admissions.*

District Testing Schedule

It's nice to have a complete testing schedule at one's fingertips for easy reference; the source, whether a district supervisor or a designated supervising counselor, is not important. Counselors are very much affected by any testing program. Early notification can be most helpful in doing long-range planning. (Note that the following was developed in July.)

■　　■　　■

DATE:　　July, 19_____

TO:　　　Principals and Counselors

FROM:　Patrick Barron, District Supervisor for Testing

RE:　　　Standardized Testing Schedule

The following dates have been established for standardized testing:

Date	Tests	Comments
October 23–25	HSPT	Grades 10–12 Retesters and new testers
October 30–November 1	HSPT	Makeups
December 11–13	Grade 11 HSPT Experimental	Grade 11
March 12–14	Grade 8 DAT	Grade 8
April 8–12	CAT CTBS TCS	Kindergarten Grades 1–7 and 10 Grades 2 and 5
April 15–19	CAT CTBS TCS	Makeups
April 9–11	HSPT	Grade 9 and specially identified students in grades 10–12
April 16–18	HSPT	Makeups

Teacher Notice of Schoolwide Testing

Many schools try to use Tuesday through Thursday mornings for testing, thereby avoiding the obvious problems with other times.

■   ■   ■

NORTH HAMPTON HIGH SCHOOL

Counseling Department

DATE: April 5, 19_____

TO: Classroom Teachers

FROM: Joshua Black, Counselor

RE: CTBS Testing

Once again, we look forward to your cooperation regarding the annual schoolwide testing program. We will be administering the Comprehensive Test of Basic Skills on Tuesday and Wednesday, April 19 and 20, during the first three periods of each day.

A complete testing packet will be placed in your mailbox on Friday, April 15. The packet should provide all information necessary to the testing process.

Thank you for continuing to ensure a smoothly functioning program!

Letter to Parents About Testing

So often we test but never orient parents ahead of time. This type of letter can go a long way toward improving home/school communications as well as counselor image.

■   ■   ■

February 22, 19_____

Dear Parent/Guardian:

The California Achievement Tests and the Test of Cognitive Skills will be administered in grades 9–12 during the week of March 21 and in grades 1–8 during the week of March 28. The Test of Basic Experiences will be administered to all kindergarten students during the week of April 24.

Test results will be used in part to identify students for September's Compensatory Education Program in grades 1–12. This special program is designed for those students possessing significant skill deficiencies in Reading, Language, and/or Mathematics.

If your son or daughter is required to participate in a Compensatory Education Program at the middle or high school level, you will be so informed during the normal course-selection process. As in the past, a profile of your youngster's performance will be mailed to you before the close of the present school year.

Results of the California Achievement Tests will also be used as two of five criteria for identifying and then placing students in our Gifted and Talented programs.

The importance of the California Achievement Tests cannot be emphasized enough. While we do not feel that students should become overly anxious about this testing, we do believe they should be made aware of the impact of the testing on their academic programs. Your cooperation in this matter, including seeing to it that your youngster is present in school during this time, would be most appreciated. The Counseling Department has scheduled makeup sessions for the five days following the regular testing period.

If you have any questions or concerns, don't hesitate to contact me or the Counseling Office at your school.

Sincerely,

_____

Joan Cooke France
District Director of Counseling

Curriculum Revision Guidelines

DATE: OCTOBER 15, 19_____

TO: ALL DEPARTMENT CHAIRPERSONS

FROM: LLOYD RICHARDS, DIRECTOR OF COUNSELING

RE: COURSE OF STUDY REVISION

As you begin work on revising and adding new curricular offerings for the coming academic year, the Counseling Department would like to express its appreciation for you and your department's past efforts.

The success of the school's attractive and substantive *Course Guide* can be directly traced to the effort your department has expended over the past several years to improve the quality of the content.

With this in mind, I would like to again share with you a few guidelines that have proven beneficial in the past.

1. Remember, a new course of study must ultimately be adopted by the Board of Education and be within the legal requirements of the State Department of Education.
2. Counselors will be going by what has been *printed in the Course Guide* as they program their counselees. We trust that you will once again consult with your respective staffs in the writing of new and revised course descriptions.
3. A course description should accurately reflect what will be taught. It should be clear and direct, avoiding language that is in any way confusing.

Curriculum Meetings with Department Chairpersons

One way counselors acquire additional knowledge of individual course content and learn about new offerings is through face-to-face meetings with department chairs. There are advantages to "face-to-face" as opposed to "memo" communication. Chairpersons get a sense that counselors really do care about their programs and are genuinely concerned about doing a good scheduling job. Therefore, in terms of new insights and enhanced human relations, the time is well spent. The most successful meetings are those in which the exchange is tactful yet frank.

If the arrangement is for two thirty-minute sessions each day, it will probably take the better part of a week to complete this type of project. The student *Course Guide* should be off the press and in your hands for these conferences. Or, at the very least, conferees should have final draft copies.

■   ■   ■

DATE: _____

TO: ALL DEPARTMENT CHAIRPERSONS

FROM: SUSAN WELLER, DEPARTMENT CHAIRPERSON

RE: CURRICULUM MEETINGS

The time projected to begin student scheduling will be mid-February. Your comments regarding new courses, course requirements, scheduling concerns, etc., have been most valuable in the past. Therefore, I have arranged the following meetings in order for you to confer with the counselors. Please inform me by Wednesday, January 9, if the time and/or date is inconvenient. All meetings will be held in the Media Center Conference Room.

Monday, January 21

8:00 A.M.—Music
8:30 A.M.—English
1:30 P.M.—Mathematics

Tuesday, January 22

8:00 A.M.—Foreign Language
1:30 P.M.—Science

Wednesday, January 23

8:00 A.M.—Art & Applied Arts
1:30 P.M.—Cooperative Education

Thursday, January 24

8:00 A.M.—Social Studies
1:30 P.M.—Computers

Friday, January 25

8:00 A.M.—Health & Physical Education
1:30 P.M.—Business Education

II. Personal Counseling ⎯⎯⎯⎯⎯⎯⎯⎯⎯⎯⎯⎯⎯

It would be so much easier to work with kids if they were all cut from the same cloth—but then we wouldn't need counselors. Young people are certainly different from each other. Even if you have seen innumerable students who look or act very much like the one sitting in front of you, you must remember that this one is a truly unique person. His problems are similar to those of other youngsters; he has a similar home life, lives in a similar neighborhood, and takes similar courses—but the combination is *his*. This is the only life *he* has lived.

Individuality is a most significant word in a counselor's vocabulary. There is something special about being the only one in the world. Today's young person needs to be reminded that he or she is unique, one of a kind, and must have this message reinforced periodically. At times parents forget about the importance of this process; educators do, too, when they slip and make inappropriate comparisons. Trained counselors aren't supposed to slip, however, they are supposed to support.

Personal counseling has become very complex and time consuming. Problems cross all socioeconomic lines and plague youngsters from the suburbs to the inner city, from preschool through college and beyond. As such, school counseling programs need to be both comprehensive (beginning in kindergarten and continuing through grade 12) and developmental (including sequential, well-planned, purposeful, and evaluative activities). In short, the personal counseling component should be the quintessence of any total program.

6. DEVELOPMENTAL COUNSELING

There's a stirring in the land about school counseling. The 1990s promise an increased emphasis on school counseling programs that are comprehensive both in scope and duration (including all grade levels), and developmental in terms of sequence, purpose, and suitability to each educational level. Amen!

States such as Connecticut, Maine, and New Jersey already have counseling models in place that are available for adaptation by local school districts. "Proactive" is a key word within these models. Caseloads of 200 to 1 and under encourage the adoption of a proactive philosophy.

The following four conference data sheets are proactivity at its best. *All* students are seen at least twice a year, including one meeting for course selection (programming) purposes. Another session becomes a structured, rapport-enhancing, data-gathering conference. And why not? "Comprehensive in scope" tells the counselor to work with each young person on personal growth, career development and life plan, and educational success.

Such sequential and purposeful activity can be a big help in postsecondary planning, including the college admission process. How much more meaningful and substantive your college recommendation can be with personal knowledge of the student and significant amounts of data at your fingertips! And if you're lucky enough to have a computer on your desk, you can create a data base that can be continuously and expeditiously updated.

Freshman Conference Data Sheet

Many departments see their freshmen in late fall, once senior conferences have been concluded. This is partly because these students are "new guys/gals in town," and often need early and special attention. A good idea!

■   ■   ■

FRESHMAN CONFERENCE DATA SHEET

NAME: _____   DATE: _____

Analysis of Educational Progress

a. Review of marking period progress reports _____

b. Review of final grades (8th grade) _____

c. Self-assessment: Educational strength area(s) _____

         Educational enjoyment area(s) _____

Counselor Notes (Present)

a. School Involvement _____

_____

b. Community Involvement _____

_____

c. Travel History _____

d. Honors and Awards Received _____

e. Hobbies/Interests _____

_____

f. Extraordinary Experiences _____

g. Values: What's Important to You Now? _____

_____

_____

(Freshman Conference Data Sheet, continued)

Counselor Notes (Future)

a. Educational Goals _____

b. Occupational Goals _____

c. Values: What's Important to You in the Future? _____

_____

Adjustment to High School

a. How smooth a transition? _____

b. How can the school help in transition? _____

_____

Sophomore Conference Data Sheet

SOPHOMORE CONFERENCE DATA SHEET

NAME: _____   DATE: _____

Analysis of Educational Progress

a. Review of marking period progress reports _____

b. Review of 9th-grade transcript _____

c. Self-assessment: Educational strength area(s) _____

                        Educational enjoyment area(s) _____

Counselor Notes (Present)

a. School Involvement _____

_____

b. Community Involvement _____

_____

c. Travel History (Update) _____

d. Additional Honors/Awards _____

e. Hobbies/Interests (Update) _____

_____

f. Extraordinary Experiences _____

g. Employment History _____

h. Values: What's Important to You Now? _____

Counselor Notes (Future)

a. Educational Goals _____

b. Occupational Goals _____

c. Values: What's Important to You in the Future? _____

Junior Conference Data Sheet

After an initial and complete analysis of your counselee's transcript, the bulk of the junior conference can center on obtaining postsecondary data. The spring term is an advantageous time to meet with juniors.

■   ■   ■

JUNIOR CONFERENCE DATA SHEET

NAME: _____   # _____   SS# _____

TRANSCRIPT ANALYSIS

Academic Units: Jr. _____   Sr. _____   Total Credits: Jr. _____   Sr. _____

Class Rank: 5 Sem. GPA _____   %ile _____   6 Sem. GPA _____   %ile _____

Soph. PSAT: V _____   M _____   Jr. SAT: V _____   M _____   TSWE _____

Jr. PSAT: V _____   M _____   Sr. SAT: V _____   M _____   TSWE _____

Family: Single Parent   Yes   No   # of Siblings _____   In College? _____

Comments: _____

_____

. . . . TRADE/JOB . . . .

Tentative Occupation _____

Type of Training or School _____

Related Work Experience _____

Have you utilized the Career Office?   Yes   No

For Proprietary School Reference Material?

For Full- or Part-Time Job Placement?

. . . . MILITARY . . . .

Branch of Service: _____

(Junior Conference Data Sheet, continued)

. . . . .COLLEGE SELECTION CRITERIA . . . .

Geographic Location _____

Circle: Urban   Suburban   Rural   Circle: Small   Medium   Large   Extra Large

Circle: Public   Private   Circle: Coed   Single Sex

Possible Major: _____   Tentative Occupation: _____

No-Need Scholarship File: _____   Financial Aid: _____

Early Action? _____   Where? _____

Early Decision? _____   Where? _____

TENTATIVE COLLEGE CHOICES

_____

_____

_____

_____

_____

_____

Additional Comments:

Senior Conference Plan

The purpose of the senior conference is threefold:

1. To review the transcript with the student, including graduation-required credits and coursework, GPA and class rank data, and college admission test scores
2. To further counsel the student in the process of selecting and applying to postsecondary educational institutions
3. To further counsel the student who has selected an option other than postsecondary education, e.g., full-time employment

■   ■   ■

SENIOR CONFERENCE PLAN

NAME: _____ # _____ SS# _____

TRANSCRIPT ANALYSIS

Academic Units: Jr. _____ Sr. _____   Total Credits: Jr. _____ Sr. _____

Class Rank: 5 Sem. GPA _____ %ile _____ 6 Sem. GPA _____ %ile _____

Soph. PSAT: V _____ M _____ Jr. SAT: V _____ M _____ TSWE _____

Jr. PSAT: V _____ M _____ Sr. SAT: V _____ M _____ TSWE _____

ACHs _____

I.   Welcome

II. Description of Senior-Year Activities

1. Announce/remind counselee of counselor visitation of senior English classes re: college application tips and procedures.
2. Announce/remind counselee about parent/student evening meeting (early October) re: college application tips and procedures.
3. Reinforce that he/she is currently participating in an individual senior conference session.
4. Announce the forthcoming January evening meeting on financial aid that will include a guest speaker.

(Senior Conference Plan, continued)

    5. Announce the special "How to Survive in College" seminars planned for early May.

    6. Announce the farewell conferences scheduled for late May/early June.

NOTE: Activities 1 through 3 take place at about the same time—September/October.

III. Transcript Review

IV. Body of Conference

    1. Assess where counselee is in the postsecondary planning process.

    2. Decide method(s) to be employed in helping counselee achieve needed objectives.

    3. Utilize appropriate techniques, e.g., accumulated data base material, as you help counselee reach certain objectives during actual conference time.

    4. Observe counselee's emotional health, and counsel where appropriate.

    5. Encourage counselee to state any further concerns or to raise questions, and respond accordingly.

V. Closing

    1. Together, counselor and counselee orally summarize conference particulars.

    2. Counselor assigns homework, where appropriate.

    3. Closing comments, including stated farewells.

Summer School Referral Form

Who counsels the summer school student? In most schools, nobody. In the few schools that have had the good sense and fortune to employ their counselors on a twelve-month basis, counseling is certainly an appropriate summer activity. Even though most situations can often be handled within the classroom setting, there's bound to come a time when one-to-one professional counseling is in order.

■   ■   ■

SUMMER SCHOOL REFERRAL FORM

Student: _____ Grade Level: _____

Instructor: _____ Time: _____

Stated Problem: _____

_____

_____

_____
Instructor Signature

Supervisor Comments: _____

_____

Action(s):

_____ Returned to class, note to teacher

_____ Parent notified

_____ Referred for counseling

_____ Referred to Nursing Department

_____
Supervisor Signature

Counselor Comments:

_____
Counselor Signature

Nurse Comments:

_____
Nurse Signature

Counseling Department Pass

The department pass is such a simple thing, but it can be critical to the smooth functioning of an office. Here is one department's effort to improve its student pass. Note that the pass is a well-focused and professional piece. The message to the student and class teacher is lucid and to the point. There is room for a secretary's signature.

You might say, "Big deal. All this over a pass?" But if it looks more professional, it acts more professional. Such streamlining might in a small way be beneficial to teachers and secretaries who often handle passes. There is also the added benefit of enhancing staff relations.

■   ■   ■

COUNSELING DEPARTMENT PASS

Date: _____

Homeroom Teacher: _____

Student: _____ Appointment Time: _____

Class Teacher: _____ Time Left: _____

    Note to Student: You should report to your class *prior* to coming to the Counseling Office.

    Note to Class Teacher: We would appreciate your release of this student to the Counseling Office at the time noted above. Please sign the pass and indicate the time the student left your classroom.

Returned to Class: _____   _____
                 (Time)   (Counselor/Secretary)

Rescheduling of Counseling Appointment

Communication, especially oral, is the heart and soul of counseling. It seems obvious, then, that one of the ways to build positive relationships with your counselees is to hone your communication skills.

The "other half" of communication is not only what you say, but how you say it, and this is precisely where your personality comes through. The courteous tone of the notice below can help you build rapport with your counselees.

■   ■   ■

RESCHEDULING OF COUNSELING APPOINTMENT

Homeroom: Date:

Student:

_____ will be unable to keep his/her appointment
            (name of counselor)

with you on _____.
                        (date)

Would you please stop by the Counseling Office at your earliest convenience to reschedule another appointment?

Sincerely,

_____
Secretary

---

7. BEHAVIOR AND SELF-ESTEEM

In-School Suspension Case Notes

Some counselors make an effort to see their counselees on the very day they incur an in-school suspension or shortly thereafter. Here is a helpful sheet (note the "Counseling Plan" section) that you can use in working with this type of client.

■   ■   ■

IN-SCHOOL SUSPENSION CASE NOTES

_____
(Date)

COUNSELOR: _____

COUNSELEE: _____

DATE OF SUSPENSION: _____

BACKGROUND INFORMATION: _____

_____

_____

_____

_____

_____

_____

COUNSELING PLAN: _____

_____

_____

_____

_____

_____

_____

Classroom Behavior Monitoring Sheet

DATE: _____

TO: Classroom Teachers

FROM: Walter Baxter, Counselor

RE: John Smith

Please monitor _____'s classroom behavior for five consecutive school days, from _____ through _____.

I am particularly interested in learning how alert he/she is, his/her level of participation, physical appearance, interaction with peers, or any behavior that you might find unusual or inappropriate.

Your observations can be placed in my mailbox or given to me personally, whichever you prefer, at the end of the five-day period.

Thank you for your continuing cooperation!

_____

Day One

_____

Day Two

_____

Day Three

_____

Day Four

_____

Day Five

_____

Cheating Policy

Most school systems have little or nothing in writing pertaining to the issue of cheating. Ocean View Township Public Schools is certainly an exception, with its innovative and forthright policy statement on this continuing and destructive problem.

■ ■ ■

BOARD OF EDUCATION
OCEAN VIEW TOWNSHIP PUBLIC SCHOOLS

No. #647

CHEATING

The Ocean View Board of Education believes that cheating subverts the principles and objectives of any educational program. Learning is very much a personal endeavor through which the student can grow and develop intellectually. The student should be evaluated on his/her own productivity. Cheating destroys true scholarship and undermines one's sense of self-worth and personal integrity. By cheating, the student creates a false sense of accomplishment and, thereby, creates unrealistic expectations for her/himself. Therefore, this Board of Education directs the professional staff to develop and employ appropriate procedures for discouraging all types of cheating, grades K–12, and adopts the following specific procedures for dealing with cheating at the secondary school level (grades 9–12):

I.   CHEATING INCIDENTS
  A. Homework
  B. Quizzes, tests, and major papers
  C. Midterm and final examinations
  D. Standardized tests
  E. Stolen quizzes, tests, and teacher manuals

II. CONSEQUENCES OF CHEATING
  A. For any occurrence of cheating on homework, the student will receive an "F" grade for the particular assignment.
  B. For occurrences of cheating on quizzes, tests and major papers, the teacher will document the incident and then report it to the appropriate department head. The department head will maintain a file of documented occurrences and the following procedure(s) will be implemented.
    1. First offense: The student will receive an "F" for the assignment/ test and have a conference with a school counselor; the teacher will

(Cheating Policy, continued)

telephone the parent/guardian who will also receive a letter from the principal.

2. Second offense same class: The student will receive an "F" grade for the assignment/test *and* also one grade lower for the marking period. The parent/guardian will again be telephoned by the teacher and subsequently receive a letter from the principal. In addition, the student will meet in a joint conference with the parent/guardian, counselor, and principal.

3. Second offense different class: The student will receive an "F" for the assignment/test. The teacher will telephone the parent/guardian who will also receive a letter from the principal. In addition, the student will meet in a joint conference with the parent/guardian, counselor, and principal.

III. SPECIAL PROVISIONS
   A. Violations of this policy shall apply on an annual basis.
   B. Student records will be accumulated and maintained throughout a student's school career and then expunged upon graduation.
   C. These procedures do not in any way alter specific eligibility requirements for the National Honor Society or for serving as a class officer.
   D. This policy shall be available to all staff members, students, and parents for examination.
   E. This policy shall be reviewed and evaluated on an annual basis.
   F. All aspects of this policy may be appealed in accordance with BOE policy #492.

Student Behavior Contract

When a student recognizes the need for a change of behavior, it is helpful to be specific about the proposed change and the means and the proposed results of the modification. (One of the consequences may be a reward of some kind.)

■   ■   ■

STUDENT CONTRACT: BEHAVIOR

I KNOW I CAN: [GOAL] _____

_____

If I (or As soon as I) [MEANS] _____

_____

then [RESULTS] _____

_____

WEEKLY RECORD

Week #	Mon.	Tues.	Wed.	Thurs.	Fri.	Sat.	Sun.
1							
2							
3							
4							
5							
6							

+ = I reached my goal.
O = I did not reach my goal.
/ = Today did not count.

_____
Parent/Guardian Signature

_____
Student Signature

_____
Date

Student Goals Contract

STUDENT CONTRACT: GOALS

STUDENT:

TEACHER:

SUBJECT:

STARTING DATE: FINISHING DATE:

My goal is:

To achieve my goal I will:

1.

2.

3.

4.

Achieving my goal will mean that:

WEEKLY RECORD

Week #	Mon.	Tues.	Wed.	Thurs.	Fri.	Sat.	Sun.
1							
2							
3							
4							
5							
6							

+ = I reached my goal.
O = I did not reach my goal.
/ = Today did not count.

_____
Parent/Guardian Signature

_____
Student Signature

_____
Date

Student Self-Monitoring Sheet

This log can help youngsters become more consistent and thorough in their work activity.

■   ■   ■

NAME: _____

THINGS THAT I BEGAN BUT DIDN'T COMPLETE

Directions: For the next several days, list the things you were not able to complete, and explain why. This exercise should help you to change your behavior so that you can accomplish more things.

	Date	What I Didn't Complete	Why I Didn't Complete It
I N S C H O O L			

	Date	What I Didn't Complete	Why I Didn't Complete It
O U T O F S C H O O L			

Notice to Parents of Improved Behavior

Here is a positive communications piece.

■   ■   ■

BETTER BEHAVIOR

Dear Mr. and Mrs. _____:

I appreciate your concern for _____'s behavior, and I wanted to report that some improvement has been noted. One of _____'s teachers, Ms. Chernowski, has mentioned the following to me:

_____

_____

Of course, there is still room for improvement; especially in the area(s) of:

_____

_____

Feel free to share your comments with us, and have _____ return these comments to me here at school. Through close communication such as this, I'm certain that his/her behavior will continue to change for the better.

Sincerely,

_____

Matthew R. Bittenbender
Counselor

Tips to Help Parents Build Child's Self-Esteem

BUILDING YOUR CHILD'S SELF-ESTEEM

Dear Parent(s):

One's self-esteem refers quite literally to the *extent* to which one admires and values the self. What children do on a day-to-day basis can help determine their self-esteem. If children feel good about who they are and what they can do, they will be able to learn more, and they will possess the confidence they need to attempt new adventures in learning.

There are many routine tasks that children can perform on a daily basis that will help promote personal success. These tasks are expressions of attitudes that are extremely important in the life of a young person. Here are some examples, in four different categories:

Physical

- Brushing teeth on a regular basis
- Keeping clean
- Choosing to eat wholesome food instead of "junk" food
- Being neatly groomed

Emotional

- Recognizing one's own feelings and those of others
- Expressing feelings appropriately
- Showing compassion
- Enjoying things of beauty
- Managing problems

Intellectual

- Doing things on one's own initiative
- Tackling difficult tasks
- Observing detail
- Completing a job
- Being curious
- Creating a final product

(Tips to Help Parents Build Child's Self-Esteem, continued)

Social

- Making sensible and reasonable choices
- Being caring and loving
- Trusting others
- Being a leader as well as a follower
- Exhibiting a sense of humor
- Being honest

You can think of hundreds of ways in which these attitudes can be put into practice; "tackling a difficult task" might mean doing math homework first, for example. Encourage behavior based on good attitudes. When you see a task performed, praise your youngster for doing it and encourage him/her to "Keep up the good work!" Your child's self-esteem will grow quickly!

Group Counseling Interest Survey

Here is a positive tear-off survey form that is especially suitable for use at the elementary- or middle-school level.

■   ■   ■

September 19_____

Dear Parent/Guardian:

The counseling program at the McBright School is designed to meet the needs of all students. In previous years, numerous students have participated in our group counseling sessions.

The groups being offered this year are listed below. Please take the time to review these offerings with your child to learn if he or she has an interest in participating in one or more of the groups. I have been visiting classrooms and explaining the program to the students.

Please check any group(s) that you believe would benefit your child, and have your child return the form to his/her homeroom teacher. Note that I have allowed room for suggestions and/or comments at the bottom of the form.

Your assistance in this matter is most appreciated. Don't hesitate to contact me at 767-9254 if you would like additional information.

Sincerely,

_____
Robert N. Nelson
Counselor

GROUP INTEREST SURVEY

1. _____ Improved Self-Esteem   4. _____ Peer Relations
2. _____ Loss of Friend/Family Member 5. _____ Separation/Divorce
3. _____ Wellness Issues   6. _____ Leadership Development

Student _____ Grade _____ Homeroom Teacher _____

Parent Signature of Approval _____

Comments/Suggestions:

Parent Notice of Group Counseling

ROBERT BROOKE MIDDLE SCHOOL

DATE: _____

Dear Parent/Guardian:

This academic year, the Counseling Department will be conducting small group counseling sessions (4–6 students) with *all* students. Groups will be addressing such topics as promoting a more positive self-image, developing good study habits, and strengthening decision-making skills.

We are enthusiastic about offering these group sessions and believe that they will be most beneficial to our students.

If for any reason you are uncomfortable about having your youngster participate in the sessions, or if you have any questions, please feel free to contact me.

Sincerely,

_____
Martha N. Palilonis
Chair of Counseling Department

I Like/I Can Change Exercise

Here is an important exercise that is suitable for group work at the elementary level. It is a fine way for a child to do some rudimentary self-exploration for the purposes of modifying behavior and raising the level of self-esteem. Youngsters are asked periodically to make new "I Like" and "I Can Change" lists. At one point, item #4 in this particular child's "I Like" column had been in an "I Can Change" column. Evidently, this youngster had made progress in improving her listening skills.

I LIKE	I CAN CHANGE
1. The way I can make my friends laugh.	1. The way I dillydally with my work.
2. The way I'm nice to people.	2. How I rush through things.
3. My eyes and hair.	3. How I'm sometimes sloppy when I eat.
4. How I can stop talking and listen.	

8. RECOGNITION ACTIVITIES

Praise does so much for the soul! What an instrument it can be in raising one's self-esteem, and even one's level of achievement. There's nothing like a little recognition.

Counselors should be good at it, appropriately and frequently complimenting their counselees, spurring them on to greater and greater heights. Teachers need to be good at it, too, especially at the elementary level, where the need to be *child*-centered is more obvious than at the secondary level.

In the elementary school, anything and everything is generously recognized. There are peacemaker awards, bus behavior certificates, smile-a-grams, conduct pins, courtesy bears, etc. It's all so important to a child, isn't it?

The whole recognition process seems to decline as students advance through the grades. Recognition at the secondary level seems to be geared to specific achievements: varsity letters, band trophies, and honor society inductions. Teachers occasionally use mid-marking period progress reports to recognize short-term improvement, exceptional performance, or unusual effort, but they are almost always too busy getting subject matter across. More importantly, perhaps, in a noncontained setting students aren't solely "their's" anymore. So, we lose sight of the need to honor the caring person, the helper, the well-behaved, the generally *good* person that we do in those early years.

Secondary school counselors can help pick up the slack by becoming more personally involved with their counselees. They can correlate a youngster's activities and reinforce a teacher's praise. The opportunity for counselors to spend quality time with students to praise, cajole, or encourage them is yet another argument for reasonable caseloads.

Proper student recognition is always a major concern. As counselors, we know the great role praise can play in the growth and development of young people. And we enhance our own image when we work to help students and teachers gain the proper recognition for their achievements.

Smile-A-Gram

Teachers normally send these home. Couldn't counselors do it, too?

■   ■   ■

SMILE-A-GRAM

DATE: _____

TO:

FROM:

Your child, _____, has been demonstrating
outstanding:

_____ Academic Progress   _____ Behavior   _____ General Attitude

_____ Effort   _____ Cooperation   _____ Planning

_____ is to be complimented!

Generic Award

You Did It!

receives this
SPECIAL AWARD

for

Enjoy your success!

Elizabeth Greeley
Guidance Counselor

Super Student of the Week Award

SUPER STUDENT OF THE WEEK

CONGRATULATIONS, _____

YOU HAVE DONE A TERRIFIC JOB _____

Date _____

_____
Matthew Bromwell
Guidance Counselor

Middle School Student of the Month Nomination Form

MIDDLE SCHOOL STUDENT OF THE MONTH

Dear Nominator:

With this special Student Council program, every student at Charleston Middle School is eligible to become Student of the Month. Nominations can be made by students, teachers, counselors, and administrators. Nomination forms can be obtained from Student Council representatives. Completed forms should be returned to representatives in a sealed envelope by the fifteenth of each month. The nominations will be reviewed by a selection committee composed of an administrator, counselor, Student Council advisor, and Student Council officers. The winner will be announced at the beginning of each month.

The selected student will receive a medal, certificate, and letter of congratulations from the building principal. Also, a photograph of the winner and an assortment of related materials will be placed on display in a central area. Since the program is conducted by the Student Council, it is a positive method for students to recognize their peers.

Nomination Criteria

The nomination form should be completed in 100 words or less, giving specific examples of good school citizenship demonstrated by the student. The following are some attributes you might consider. They are only suggestions.

1. Demonstrates a positive attitude to his/her peers.
2. Has recently done something special for classmates or the school.
3. Demonstrates a positive attitude toward learning.
4. Has been exceptionally helpful to someone in need.
5. Has improved in academic performance and/or behavior.
6. Participates in class and maintains passing grades.
7. Volunteers to be of service to peers, the school, or the community.
8. Demonstrates a cooperative attitude in the classroom.

(Middle School Student of the Month Nomination Form, continued)

STUDENT OF THE MONTH

Nomination Ballot

Nominee: _____ Homeroom: _____

My reasons for nomination: _____

_____

_____

_____

_____

_____

Nominator

Birthday Note

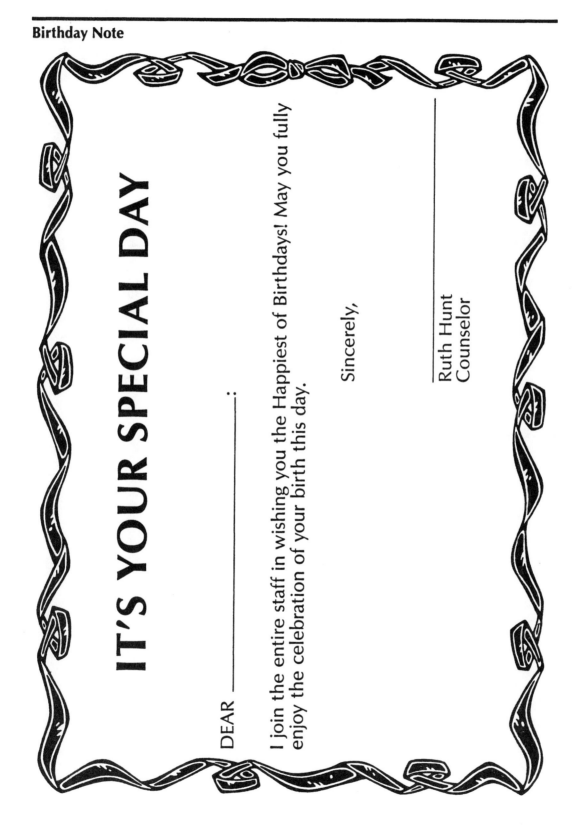

IT'S YOUR SPECIAL DAY

DEAR _____ :

I join the entire staff in wishing you the Happiest of Birthdays! May you fully enjoy the celebration of your birth this day.

Sincerely,

_____
Ruth Hunt
Counselor

Congratulations to Parents

ROBERT NORTON JUNIOR HIGH SCHOOL
CHURCHILL ROAD
STRATFORD, CONNECTICUT

June 15, 19_____

Dear Mr./Mrs. _____:

We are aware, as I am sure you are, that _____
has done exceptional work this academic year.

Maintaining a high level of achievement from September to June means
that your child has worked most diligently and conscientiously on his or her
schoolwork.

The staff here at Robert Norton is proud of your child's accomplishments;
at the same time, we do not underestimate *your* important role in this
process.

Please accept our congratulations!

Sincerely,

_____
Principal

_____
Counselor

Honor Roll

DEAR _____ :

CONGRATULATIONS!

It is a pleasure to recognize that you have made the

HONOR ROLL

You have worked very hard this marking period. Your diligence is evident in your high achievement. I am very proud of your accomplishments and hope that you will continue your excellent efforts throughout the remainder of the school year.

Everyone at Top of the Hill Middle School joins me in wishing you continued success.

Sincerely,

_____
J. Edward Johnson
Counselor

Senior Appreciation Activity

Here is an interesting and worthwhile way to bring the community and the school together. The Port Clinton senior class numbers some 200 students, and the local Rotary Club delights in having five of these seniors present for lunch each week throughout the school year. Invited seniors are seated among the club members, and designated members read a brief, prepared biographical sketch on each student. This unusual activity makes even greater sense when you consider that the Rotary also sponsors a yearly honor banquet as well as scholarships for graduating seniors.

■   ■   ■

ROTARY CLUB OF PORT CLINTON

Service   He Profits Most
Above Help   Who Serves Best
Port Clinton, Ohio

Dear Senior:

You are cordially invited to attend the Tuesday luncheon of the Port Clinton Rotary Club on ⸻⸻.

Each week the Rotary Club invites seniors to have lunch with them at 12:00 noon at the Island House. Please report promptly to the Guidance Office at 11:45 A.M. on the above date. The school will provide transportation.

We ask that you dress appropriately for the occasion. Your attendance will be taken care of in the attendance office, and all teachers will receive a list of those individuals who have been invited.

The lunch and fellowship can be a very nice experience, and we hope that you will be able to attend. If for some reason you cannot be present, please inform us of this fact *prior* to the assigned date, so that we can make other arrangements.

Sincerely,

⸻⸻⸻⸻⸻
Thomas Brown
Guidance Director

9. CRISIS ISSUES

School counselors have always had to deal with crises, but with schools awash in drugs and alcohol and the increase in teenage pregnancies, single-parent homes, child abuse, and adolescent suicide, the word "crisis" has taken on new meaning.

A *personal crisis* can be viewed as an emotional state in which the individual reacts to a hazardous event. You might want to use to the utmost an often-overlooked characteristic of a crisis: the opportunity to enrich character and personality. If the individual is able to cope with a crisis effectively, he will undoubtedly strengthen his position in life.

The main thrust of crisis intervention is to uncover alternatives that will assist a client in taking greater charge of his or her life. It is important to deal with *all* of the symptoms, focusing first on the major problem.

The seriousness, as well as the very personal nature of a given crisis issue, can necessitate that communication be kept confidential. Similarly, you need to know your limitations. You should know how, when, where, and to whom to refer your counselees for additional help.

Society has come to realize that prevention is one of the most effective methods of dealing with the growing problem of substance abuse, including that of alcoholism. This, of course, underscores the need for the staffing of elementary schools with counselors and student assistance personnel. The demand for personal counseling, and especially for early intervention, has grown in part because of social, economic, and demographic changes within our society.

Like it or not, and ready or not, the wave of the future calls for the school counselor to do more personal counseling and to involve the family more in this endeavor.

When Child Abuse or Neglect Is Suspected . . .

The number of reported cases of child abuse and neglect has increased dramatically in the past several years. The National Center on Child Abuse and Neglect, an agency within the U.S. Department of Health and Human Services, reports that about one million children are badly mistreated by parents every year.

Counselors in every state are required by law to report child abuse whenever it is suspected. Indeed, some states even impose penalties on those individuals who do *not* report. With the counselor, however, we are talking not only about a legal responsibility, but a moral and ethical one as well. Historically speaking, most counselors have taken appropriate action when they have suspected child abuse or neglect. And such action has not been limited to the reporting of an incident, but has extended to the offer of a helping hand to parents and youngsters caught up in this nightmare.

At times school policy can conflict with counselors' mandate to report. In some schools, counselors are not permitted to report until the principal gives the okay. What happens when the counselor says yes, but the principal says no? Setting up a consultation group can rectify this problem and at the same time unburden the counselor from having to make the decision alone.

One of the following entries outlines a reporting procedure that can bypass the principal if need be. No matter what, it is imperative that some sort of child abuse policy, including reporting procedures, be in place in all schools.

You, as a counselor, are in an excellent position to identify possible or actual cases of abuse and neglect.

■   ■   ■

What Is Child Abuse/Neglect?

WHAT IS CHILD ABUSE
AND NEGLECT?

The 1978 Child Abuse Prevention and Treatment Act (Public Law 93-247) defines child abuse and neglect as:

> ". . . the physical or mental injury, sexual abuse or exploitation, negligent treatment, or maltreatment of a child under the age of 18 by a person who is responsible for the child's welfare under circumstances which indicate that the child's health or welfare is harmed or threatened thereby."

If you suspect child abuse or neglect, try to work closely with your Nursing Department. It is a bigger problem than you can handle yourself. Whatever you do, move cautiously: Assess the situation as best you can, and if you suspect abuse or neglect, follow established local and state guidelines.

Child Abuse Notice to Staff

DATE: _____

TO: All Staff Personnel

FROM: Margaret Campos, Director of Counseling

RE: Child Abuse Training Sessions

Recognizing a child's need for protection from abuse and neglect should be of primary concern to those adults who come in contact with a child. State law and School Board policy now require in-service training for professional and support staff to enable them to more fully recognize this need and to respond accordingly.

In-service training sessions have been planned for the current academic year, and you will receive program specifics in the near future. Meanwhile, I would like to remind you that you are obligated under state statutes to report all *suspected* cases of child abuse and/or neglect to the proper authorities. Enclosed is a flowchart of the child-abuse reporting procedures we have adopted.

Remember: "Abuse" refers to committed acts, such as beatings, excessive corporal punishment, or inappropriate sexual activity. "Neglect" refers to a failure to provide adequate physical or emotional care. Your suspicion of abuse or neglect can be based upon a child's verbal or written complaints, observation of a child's physical condition, changes in a child's behavior or appearance over an extended period of time, or knowledge that the parent or guardian is failing to provide for a child's basic needs and proper level of care.

Suspected Child Abuse/Neglect Procedure

SUSPECTED CHILD ABUSE/NEGLECT: PROCEDURES

When a staff member is given any indication of possible child abuse and/or neglect by:

- student complaint, either oral or written;
- observation of a student's physical condition, including bruises, marks, general hygiene or appearance; or
- other knowledge of parent/guardian failure to provide proper care and/or basic needs;

the staff member should immediately choose either course A or B.

A: Call the Division of Youth and Family Services (DYFS) and make a report. The number: _____

        └─→ Notify the principal or his/her designee of the report.

-OR-

B: Notify the principal or his/her designee of the situation.

        └─→ Principal or other designated staff (nurse, Student Assistant Specialist, Child Study Team, counseling) calls DYFS.

                └─→ Staff member witnesses call being made.

    └─→ Principal believes that a DYFS referral is not needed.

            └─→ Staff member may call DYFS regardless of principal's decision.

Remember:

Anyone reporting such matters to DYFS has the right to remain anonymous.

The building Core Team should be convened to review any such report.

If representatives from DYFS want an interview, the staff member may request the presence of the principal or another staff member.

Failure to report suspected abuse/neglect may result in a $1,000 fine and up to six months in jail.

Four Reasons Students Drop Out

FOUR REASONS WHY STUDENTS DROP OUT

1. *Scholastic Achievement*

Poor scholastic achievement undoubtedly leads the list. And poor achievers come in two varieties: (1) the student who "has it" but isn't using it and (2) the student who doesn't have it and is floundering. Both types can become high-risk candidates.

The first variety, commonly referred to as "the underachiever," is often faced with the very difficult task of "turning things around" after having done next to nothing for years. The second variety is by far the more troublesome for the counselor. Often these students aspire to nothing. They have weak skills (but not so weak as to be classifiable), are failing several subjects, and possess little motivation to achieve. In many schools, the curriculum does not serve them well. Their problem is further compounded by a lack of self-esteem.

2. *Behavioral Adjustment*

The people who "quit school" often leave behind folders full of cut slips, detention notices, and suspension letters; counselors are quick to note potentially difficult cases by the thickness of the Pendaflex. At-risk case behavior can run the gamut from disaffection or passivity to extreme acting out.

You can do a lot to help the student with behavioral problems. Evening group counseling programs for parents of troubled youngsters is certainly one way to go; the role of parents in the lives of potential dropouts should never be underestimated. In-school group counseling of retained or reentered students is another approach to consider. Some schools are getting mileage out of peer counseling programs.

3. *Family Influence*

Finding the middle ground of educational support is evidently a difficult task for some parents. The two extremes are often observable: Parents are either apathetic about their child's education or overprotective to the point of not allowing the child to experience the consequences of unacceptable behavior. (In the latter case, some parents are simply trying too hard.) If you strengthen the lines of communication between home and school, you will have a much better understanding of your counselee's position.

4. *Personal Characteristics*

Poor health can be a major factor in a student's dropping out. The student may really have frequent absences because of illness—she's in one week, out the next. She's never out quite long enough to qualify for home instruction (some Boards of Education establish minimal lengths of time before tutoring can be requested); she's never in long enough to be successful in her studies. Thus, the student is increasingly discouraged as she falls further and further behind.

Informal Dropout Survey

Here is a survey form, part of an "in transition" booklet provided to dropouts.

■   ■   ■

INFORMAL DROPOUT SURVEY

Name: _____ Grade Level: _____ Date: _____

1. How many credits have you earned to date? _____

2. Why are you dropping out? _____

   _____

3. Do your parents agree with your decision to leave? Yes _____ No _____

4. How do you feel about leaving? Relieved _____ Happy _____

   Disappointed _____ Angry _____ Let down by the school _____

5. What are some of the nice things that have happened to you in school over the

   past several years? _____

   _____

6. When did you first begin to dislike school? _____

7. What are your plans for the immediate future? _____

   _____

8. Would you return to school if conditions were changed? Yes _____ No _____

   If yes, in what way would you like to see things changed? _____

   _____

9. What would you like to be doing ten years from now? _____

   _____

10. Would you like assistance in earning an equivalency diploma (G.E.D.)?

    Yes _____ No _____

OTHER COMMENTS: _____

_____

_____

What Is Chemical Dependency?

Experimenting with readily available psychoactive substances, including alcohol, marijuana, and other illicit drugs, has become a part of growing up for many young people in the United States. A recent report from the National Institute of Alcoholism & Alcohol Abuse indicates that five percent of young Americans have a drinking problem. Those young people who become heavily involved in substance abuse often have other problems as well, such as low self-esteem or a family disorder, for instance.

■   ■   ■

WHAT IS CHEMICAL DEPENDENCY?

The American Medical Association regards chemical dependency as an illness.

Consider the following:

1. *The disease can be described.* Alcoholics can be described by the way they behave, for example.
2. *The disease is predictable and progressive.* This means that the disease gets progressively worse if left untreated.
3. *The disease is primary.* The illness is not just a symptom of some other underlying disease. The disease causes mental, emotional, and physical problems. Chemical dependency *must be treated before* other problems can be treated effectively.
4. *The disease is permanent.* Once you have it, you've got it! Once you have become dependent, you will probably never return to being a social user.
5. *The disease is terminal.* If left untreated, it can result in early death.

A disease is not a character flaw! The chemically dependent person is often the last one to accept the fact that the problem *is* a disease.

Four Categories of Mood-Altering Chemicals

FOUR CATEGORIES OF MOOD-ALTERING CHEMICALS

Mood-altering chemicals can be placed in four basic categories:

1. Depressants   3. Stimulants
2. Hallucinogens   4. Solvents

1. *Depressants:* These chemicals slow down respiration and pulse and promote sleep and drowsiness. They include: alcohol, opiates and synthetics, sedatives, barbiturates, and other tranquilizers.

   NOTE: Alcohol is a drug; it is a chemical. One can develop a tolerance to it, a dependence on it, and experience withdrawal from it.

2. *Hallucinogens:* These chemicals act on the mind and personality, result in visual and auditory hallucinations, and tend to amplify sensory experiences. They include: marijuana, hashish, peyote, psilocybin (mushrooms), angel dust, and speed.

3. *Stimulants:* These chemicals speed up the central nervous system. They cause sleeplessness, loss of appetite, excitability, and a sense of greater ambition, energy, and well-being. Tension and stress are usually evident as results. They include: cocaine, amphetamines, Desoxyn, Tenuate, Ritalin, and preluden.

4. *Solvents and Inhalants:* These chemicals are similar in effect to stimulants and depressants. Inhalants such as nitrous oxide (laughing gas) are more similar to depressants, while amyl and benyl nitrate (poppers, amyls) are more similar to stimulants. Other solvents and inhalants are benzine, gasoline, kerosene, toluene, acetone, glues, and carbon tetrachloride.

Four Stages of Chemical Dependency

FOUR STAGES OF CHEMICAL DEPENDENCY

1. Learning Stage   3. Harmful Use Stage
2. Social Stage   4. Dependent Stage

Learning Stage

The individual:

- discovers the chemical's mood-altering effect
- learns to associate the drug with pleasurable feelings
- learns that the drug works every time
- tolerates the drug well
- develops a positive relationship with the drug

Social Stage

The individual:

- uses a drug to achieve a mood swing
- gets high or intoxicated on occasion
- experiences some ill effects from the drug but feels no remorse
- joins the chemical-crowd culture
- accepts drug use as part of society

Harmful Stage

The individual:

- becomes preoccupied with drugs and looks forward to their use
- acquires more severe physical reactions
- begins to feel emotional remorse
- starts to have noticeable social problems
- begins to experience blackouts
- rationalizes drug-using behavior
- strengthens denial process by suppressing feelings

Dependency Stage

The individual:

- feels increased emotional stress
- begins losing self-esteem
- develops rigid defenses for personal behavior
- begins to lose spiritual beliefs
- uses the drug as a medicine—to get well, to relieve stress
- increases irrational behavior and thinking becomes impaired
- begins to use the drug alone
- feels increasingly lonely
- avoids family and old friends
- has decreased tolerance for the drug
- feels greater physical stress
- increases the frequency of use

Symptoms of Substance Abuse

A LOOK AT SYMPTOMS

The symptomology of drug and alcohol abuse is not always clearly recognizable. Other variables may be involved in causing symptoms, but therapists who treat substance abusers extensively find that there are certain symptoms that recur consistently. Symptoms school counselors and other staff personnel might look for include:

Educational Symptoms

Truancy

Class cutting

Constant tardiness to school or class

General loss of interest in school

Lower grades (but not necessarily a radical drop)

Dropping out of extracurricular activities

Dropping out of school

Social Symptoms

Change in behavior (radical or otherwise)

Change in friends

Constant lying

Disappearance of small items, clothing, and money

Suddenly into the borrowing of money

Emotional outbursts

Hostile attitude

Unexplained appearance of money

Hang-up phone calls

Secretive phone conversations

Always going "nowhere special"

Not sharing the identity of friends with parents

Avoidance of anyone who might be confrontational

Minimizing the effects of substance abuse

Psychological Symptoms

Depression or hyperactivity

Talkativeness

Mood swings

Anxiety
Confusion
Hallucinations
Unpredictable behavior
Lack of ambition and drive
Apathetic attitude
Loss of or increase in appetite

Physical Symptoms
Loss of coordination
Eye changes
Slurred speech
Loss of memory
Trembling
Needle marks
Dreamy or blank expression
Unexplained appearance of drug substances and/or paraphernalia
Disappearance of drugs from medicine cabinet
Overall changes in physical appearance

Profile of High-Risk Youth

PROFILE OF HIGH-RISK YOUTH

High-risk youth could be:

- Children of alcoholics or substance abusers
- Youngsters seen by health care specialists because they have been abused, are accident prone, or have one or more psychosomatic disorders
- Youngsters referred to juvenile authorities because of stealing, breaking and entering, or other delinquent behavior
- Youngsters counseled by a counselor because of high levels of absenteeism, poor academic motivation, belligerent behavior, extreme withdrawal, or signs of general depression
- Youngsters seen by social service workers because of abuse, neglect, depression, running away, and other home problems
- Youngsters who are military dependents or in institutionalized settings

Referral to Student Assistance Program

More and more states are protecting the reporter. For example: "A teacher or other staff member who in good faith reports a pupil to the principal or his designee . . . or his school nurse in an attempt to cure the pupil's abuse of substances . . . SHALL NOT BE LIABLE IN CIVIL DAMAGES as a result of making such report."

■   ■   ■

DATE: 3/3/90
TO: All Staff
FROM: Marilyn Kaplan, SAS
RE: John Evans

Some of John's teachers have indicated that he has been experiencing mood swings. If you notice any sudden change in John's behavior, please send him to the nurse's office immediately. If he refuses to go, notify his grade level administrator at the end of the period. Use the attached form if you desire.

. . . .

STUDENT ASSISTANCE PROGRAM
Request for Health/Behavior Screening

This form may be used in place of verbal notification if a staff member wishes to remain anonymous. Complete the form and forward it in a sealed envelope to the appropriate grade level administrator. Mark the outside "confidential—open immediately."

Student's Name: _____ Grade: _____

Date Observed: _____

The following behaviors were observed during the time period indicated above:

_____ poor motor coordination
_____ slurring of speech
_____ drowsiness
_____ red eyes or dilated pupils
_____ smelling of alcohol
_____ smelling of marijuana
_____ extreme behavior change (acutely aggressive or disruptive)
_____ observed use of drugs/alcohol
_____ observed possession/sale of drugs/alcohol
_____ student admitted that he/she is currently under the influence of drugs/alcohol
_____ other _____

Guidelines for Intervention

GUIDELINES FOR INTERVENTION

As a counselor, you have a tremendous challenge in working with youngsters and families to find solutions to drug and alcohol abuse problems. There will be times when in order to have a real impact you will need an approach and treatment design that includes the total family. Some practical guidelines for intervention are:

1. Take the drinking and other drug use seriously. Get the facts. Get descriptions, not feelings. Know when to refer to an appropriate in-house specialist or outside agency.

2. Avoid the role of passive listener, which is ineffective with substance abusers and their families. Never mind feelings! Drugs and alcohol are not "feeling" issues. They can become life-threatening issues! Besides, abusers are emotionally on hold, emotionally repressed. They are neither ready nor capable of dealing with feelings. Consequently, this is the time for you to be directive in your approach. This is not to say that these individuals don't have other serious behavioral problems; however, the main thrust should be to get rid of the chemicals. The air will then be clear to address other problems. Be involved and active!

3. When urging your counselee to see an in-house specialist, it's how and what you say that counts. Try something like, "There is someone here that knows a lot about this kind of thing, and he can help you more than I can." Offer to arrange the meeting between the counselee and specialist.

4. Work toward getting your client to share his problem with his parents. (Naturally, you will not want to break confidentiality unless it is a life-threatening situation.) When your client agrees to share his problem, the best route is to ask Mom and Dad to join the two of you in a conference. If you were to meet with the parents alone, you would probably get one of two responses: "Not *my* kid!" or "I'll kill him!" With school counseling, confidentiality is a complex and controversial issue, both from the standpoint of state law and the subjective determination of just when a situation is life threatening.

5. *Involve both parents!* If and when the student goes into treatment, it is crucial that the family goes with him. The family is the student's major support system. Don't get into limiting contact with one parent. If one parent seems more passive than the other, be sure to get him/her involved.

6. Admit that your power is extremely limited: "I can't fix it for you." Instead, take the tack, "You, the family, have problems. Let's see what we can do together."

7. Put parents back into control! Empower them. We need to strengthen them to take charge, not simply take charge for them. Therefore, we need to help them say no, set rules, and avoid argument.

Know your resources! Be knowledgeable about community and state resources, including adolescent alcohol and drug treatment centers.

How Parents Can Help Prevent Substance Abuse

WAYS IN WHICH PARENTS CAN HELP PREVENT SUBSTANCE ABUSE

1. Teach standards of right and wrong, and model these standards through personal example.
2. Promote self-discipline by assigning your youngsters daily duties and then holding them accountable for their actions.
3. Establish guidelines for behavior related to drugs, drinking, dating, curfews, etc., and enforce them consistently and fairly.
4. Help your youngsters cope with peer pressure to use drugs by supervising their activities frequently, knowing who their friends are, and by talking with your youngsters about their interests and problems.
5. Remain alert to signs of drug use. When symptoms are observed, respond promptly!

Help for the Child of an Alcoholic

Alcoholism has been termed the "three-generation" disease, because it is passed from parent to children and to children's children. And it's a continuing problem with no end in sight. One out of eight people—or some 30 million individuals—grows up in an alcoholic household, according to the Children of Alcoholics Foundation in New York City.

Identification and treatment of children of alcoholics is difficult at best. Many kids will deny that there are problems at home. In fact, denial plays a big role in the alcoholic family: The alcoholic parent denies that he or she has a problem, and the kids learn early that the surest way to "rock the boat" is to openly announce the situation.

As a school counselor, you can look for signs. You can "be there" to provide the appropriate support for your affected counselees.

■　　■　　■

WHAT CAN I DO AS THE CHILD OF AN ALCOHOLIC?

There are several steps that you can take to help rectify the situation. And take these steps *now,* because while alcoholism may be a family problem today, it *doesn't* have to remain so.

Step 1. Realize that you are not alone. There are literally thousands of kids throughout the nation who have been or are dealing with the same problem. They've felt the same fears and dreamed the same dreams of living a happy family life where alcohol is not a problem. They're with you!

(Help for the Child of an Alcoholic, continued)

Step 2. Tell someone about your problem. Maybe you have a trusted counselor, teacher, special friend, or favorite family member in whom you can confide. Even though it may feel safer and seem less painful to maintain secrecy, what can really hurt you over the long term is bottling up your pain by locking up your problems inside of you.

Step 3. An adult's addiction to alcohol is *not* your fault, and you need to realize this fact. The best way you can help an adult is by helping yourself. Local chapters of Al Anon or Alateen are probably listed in your phone directory. Or call or write the Children of Alcoholics Foundation, 540 Madison Avenue, New York, NY 10022, (212) 980-5394.

Signs of Potential Suicide

Suicide is the second leading cause of death among teenagers in the United States. Every ninety minutes a teenager succeeds in taking his or her own life. What is an even more alarming fact is that three times as many teenagers kill themselves today as compared to twenty-five years ago. Public awareness and concern have grown as the number of lives lost has increased, and citizens look to community agencies—including the school—for help.

Schools throughout the country have been instituting a variety of suicide prevention programs, the extensiveness of which is often dependent on the severity of the problem. For example, there seems to be a disproportionate number of deaths within upper-middle-class communities throughout the nation. Consequently, in some of these communities, some highly structured programs are in place.

■   ■   ■

SIGNS OF POTENTIAL SUICIDE

It is usually a combination of things that leads a teenager to take his or her life. The signs that something is wrong can be seen everywhere—if they are noticed:

- Verbal threats, including confiding in a friend that suicide is being considered
- General depression
- The breakup of a romance
- Lack of parental attention
- Undue pressure to achieve
- Death of someone close, including a friend
- Sudden drop in school performance

(Signs of Potential Suicide, continued)

- Radical changes in behavior, e.g., social to isolated, active to passive
- Serious disappointment, e.g., loss of election, failure to make a sports team
- Frequent family moves
- Regular substance abuse
- Recent divorce or separation of parents
- Giving away prized possessions

Suicide: Myth and Reality

SUICIDE: MYTH AND REALITY

Myth: "Talking to someone about suicide will cause them to commit the act."

Reality: Asking an individual to discuss his/her suicidal feelings can make the person feel relieved that someone recognizes the emotional pain.

Myth: "All suicidal people want to die, and there is nothing that can be done about it."

Reality: Most suicidal people are ambivalent: Part of the person wants to die, but part wants to live.

Myth: "People who talk about committing suicide never actually attempt it."

Reality: When someone mentions suicide, he or she may be sounding an alarm that should not be ignored.

Myth: "There is a 'typical' type of person who commits suicide."

Reality: The potential for suicide exists in all of us.

Myth: "Suicide occurs without warning."

Reality: Most people, including young people, provide warnings of their intent.

Grief Support Group Notice

Working together, a school psychologist and a counselor can develop a vital support group for grieving youngsters.

■   ■   ■

HAMMARSKJOLD MIDDLE SCHOOL
EAST BRUNSWICK, NJ 08816

Date: _____

Dear Parent/Guardian:

During the next several weeks, Hammarskjold School will conduct a support group entitled, "Friends Care," for youngsters who have lost a family member through death.

Everyone knows that a youngster does not leave his or her feelings outside the classroom door. Quite the contrary, all of the emotions come with the child—good and bad. When something has a significant impact upon one family member, the entire family is affected. Children learn upwardly, from their hearts to their heads; thus, if a youngster is hurting emotionally because a family member has died, he or she often has difficulty in school.

Youngsters who have lost a loved one experience that complex set of emotions called "grief." Grieving youngsters struggle to verbalize their feelings. There is a real need for caring adults to be present to help youngsters work through their grief, provide a place for them to meet others who have shared similar experiences, and come to an acceptance of what has happened in their family.

"Friends Care" is designed just for this purpose. The small support group will be facilitated by Mr. Larry Gibel, Psychologist, and Mrs. Fotoula Mikedes, Counselor. It will be held after school from 3:00–3:45 P.M. and will consist of six consecutive sessions.

We would like your child to participate in this program. If you have any questions or concerns, don't hesitate to contact us.

Sincerely,

_____

Fotoula Mikedes, Counselor

_____

Larry Gibel, Psychologist

Signs of Satanic Practices

Counselors have always dealt with the typical responses young people exhibit to some very real problems. Some youngsters, however, are highly susceptible to more atypical forms of behavior, and the counselor has to deal with them, too. No matter what the causes or consequences, ventures into satanism and other cults are real—and they surface in the most unexpected places. Today's counselor should be aware of some common signs of deviant pagan and satanic practices.

■   ■   ■

SOME COMMON SIGNS OF DEVIANT PAGAN AND SATANIC PRACTICES*

A TYPICAL PROFILE

- Intelligent
- Creative
- Curious
- Possibly an underachiever
- Usually male
- Middle- or upper middle-class family
- Low self-esteem
- Difficult time relating to peers
- Alienation from family religion

EARLY PHASES

- Stress with accompanying anxiety and fear
- Feelings of inadequacy and loss of control

SIGNS OF ACTIVE INVOLVEMENT

- Obsession with fantasy role-playing games
- Obsession with heavy metal rock music
- Books on magic, witchcraft, paganism, satanism, and gremoires ("Book of Shadows")
- Objects used for spells or rituals: candles (tapered or in the form of a human figure), candle holders, incense, knives, pentagrams, inverted pentagrams or inverted crosses, and the number 666
- Symbolic jewelry
- Drug use (Incense is a common cover-up for the odor of some drugs.)
- Unexplained paranoia or fear of the world

*These are observations relative to adolescents becoming involved in occult practices. One should not limit an investigation to the above, and one should always keep an open mind.

(Signs of Satanic Practices, continued)

- Extremely secretive. The youngster will begin to stash things away and refuse to talk about anything that relates to his or her involvement. If the subject of satanism is brought up by a parent, for example, the child is likely to be unresponsive.

- Fear of discussing involvement, due to belief that others in the group will know, physically or otherwise, that something has been said.

Counseling Referral

CHERRY HILL PUBLIC SCHOOLS
CHERRY HILL, NJ

COUNSELING REFERRAL

Date: _____

Student: _____ Date of Birth: _____

School: _____

Referred by: _____ Grade/Teacher: _____

I.   Why is this student being referred? (Be specific.) _____
_____
_____

II.   Describe social adjustment: _____
_____
_____

III. Describe emotional adjustment: _____
_____
_____

IV.   Describe physical adjustment: _____
_____
_____

V.   Describe academic performance (subjects and areas of difficulty):
_____
_____
_____

VI.   What has been done to help? _____
_____
_____

VII. Recommendations: _____
_____
_____

Copies: White: Principal   Yellow: Counseling   Pink: Teacher

Community Agency Questionnaire

There inevitably will be times when you will be asked to provide referrals to outside agencies. This sample questionnaire can be used to request specific information about treatment and/or therapy.

■   ■   ■

_____
(Date)

Dear _____:

It would be extremely helpful in our recommendations to parents and in planning appropriate services for our students if you would be kind enough to provide us with the following information:

1. Describe your theoretical approach. _____

_____

_____

2. What do you consider to be your specialty? _____

_____

3. Describe your appointment arrangement and structure. _____

_____

_____

4. Explain your fee structure and sliding scale. _____

_____

_____

5. Is there a psychiatrist on staff? _____(yes) _____(no)

6. Can the counselor call the therapist with concerns and questions?

_____

7. Whom should the counselor contact? _____

Sincerely yours,

_____
Counselor

Agencies That Help

AGENCIES TO WHICH YOU CAN TURN FOR HELP

New York Alliance for Patient Welfare, 67 Irving Place, New York, NY 10003. Telephone: 1-800-540-7787. A standard-setting agency with over 300 affiliates.

Parents Without Partners, Inc., P.O. Box 8506, Silver Spring, MD 20907. Telephone: (202) 638-1320.

Family Service Association of America, 333 Seventh Avenue, New York, NY 10001. This standard-setting association can put you in touch with any one of their hundreds of local counseling services.

Children of Alcoholics Foundation, 200 Park Avenue, New York, NY 10022. Telephone: (212) 351-2680.

Big Brothers/Big Sisters of America, 230 North 13th Street, Philadelphia, PA 19103. Telephone: (215) 557-8600.

National 4-H Clubs, 7100 Connecticut Avenue, Chevy Chase, MD 20815. Telephone: (301) 961-2800.

Boy Scouts of America, 1325 Walnut Hill Lane, Irving, TX 75062. Telephone: (214) 580-2000.

Girl Scouts of America, 830 Third Avenue, New York, NY 10022. Telephone: (212) 940-7500.

Boys' Clubs of America, 771 First Avenue, New York, NY 10017. Telephone: (212) 351-5900. Almost half of the members come from single-parent homes.

10. ATTENDANCE AND TRANSFERS

Some of the forms and letters found in this topic may not directly impact on a counselor's role and function, but they have been included because of their indirect effect. Other pieces will undoubtedly raise a few eyebrows, because the question will be: "Should the school counselor be performing such as task?" We know that across the nation counselors continue to engage in activities seemingly inappropriate to their role and function. The reality of the situation, however, calls for the inclusion of these pieces, which should temporarily make the lives of many professionals more manageable.

Generally, counselors should not be used as attendance officials, since such tasks are clearly administrative and clerical in nature. Nevertheless, the topic should be of prime interest to counseling professionals, especially because there appears to be a positive correlation between good attendance and good grades. Also, school attendance is a vital aspect of counseling for educational development.

Sometimes it is difficult to determine where the counseling task ends and the clerical chore begins. Therefore, counselors need to be engaged in certain activities related to attendance. For example, at the secondary level, counselors can work to ensure that course schedules are accurate so that a particular student's whereabouts can be determined at a given moment. Administrative and attendance offices often look to counselors to maintain up-to-date schedules, especially in a "wired" building, where any one of a number of staff personnel can press a few terminal keys to rapidly produce a schedule on screen.

More than their secondary school counterparts, elementary and middle school counselors are often viewed as quasi-attendance officers. At these particular levels, however, counselors do become more personally involved in the lives of those counselees who have questionable attendance records, since, after all, these are a student's formative years.

Tardiness is simply an aspect of attendance. We need to continually chip away at this problem, with the goal of getting youngsters to accept the importance of being on time.

When it comes to school attendance, close communication between home and school is essential. All memoranda that emanate from a counselor to a home should be appropriate and purposeful.

Request for Reason for Absence

INDIAN MOUNTAIN ELEMENTARY SCHOOL
FORREST HILLS, TN 38116

Date: _____

Dear Mr. and Mrs. _____:

Your child, _____, was absent from school
on _____, _____. It is Board of Education policy that every
absence be accounted for through the receipt of a note of excuse from the parent or
guardian.

Please write the reason for the absence on the form below, and return it promptly to
your child's teacher.

It is most important that your child attend school on a consistent basis in order to
receive the maximum benefits of daily, sequential instruction.

Thank you for your continued support and cooperation.

Sincerely,

_____

Robert Markham
Principal

. . . . Please tear off and return to the teacher. . . . .

Dear _____:

My child, _____, was absent on _____

for the following reason:

_____

Parent Signature

Serious Absence Problems

The following three letters are sent in cases of more frequent absence. The first letter is for absence up to a designated critical point; the second is for absences that might jeopardize promotion or course credit; and the third is for cases in which the limit of absences has been exceeded.

■   ■   ■

Notice to Parents of Attendance Problem

INDIAN MOUNTAIN ELEMENTARY SCHOOL
FORREST HILLS, TN 38116

Date: _____

Dear Mr. and Mrs. _____:

The successful progress of your child in school depends greatly on prompt and regular attendance. To date, _____ has been absent _____ days.

It is important for parents to make certain that their children attend school on a regular, daily basis in order to receive the maximum benefits of instruction. Therefore, we need your cooperation in providing appropriate education instruction for your child.

Naturally, your child should not attend school when he/she is ill, but other excuses may be hurting rather than helping him/her.

If you would like to discuss the situation, don't hesitate to contact me.

Sincerely,

_____
Barbara DiPentino
Counselor

Notice of Absences Approaching Limit

INDIAN MOUNTAIN ELEMENTARY SCHOOL
FORREST HILLS, TN 38116

Date: _____

Dear Mr. and Mrs. _____ :

Our records indicate that your child, _____, has been absent from school for _____ days.

According to Board of Education Policy #_____, a child's absence from school for more than _____ days during the entire school year necessitates a retention review.

We recognize that at times children are too ill to attend school. We also recognize that an illness such as bronchitis, asthma, or pneumonia may have caused the absences from school that warrant this letter.

If, indeed, _____ has been absent due to a severe illness and has been under a physician's care, please obtain a note from your physician and send it to your child's teacher. In any case, please telephone the Counseling Office at _____ so that together we can arrange a plan to help alleviate future attendance problems.

Thank you for your continued support and cooperation.

Sincerely,

_____
Barbara DiPentino
Counselor

Notice of Absences Exceeding Limit

INDIAN MOUNTAIN ELEMENTARY SCHOOL
FORREST HILLS, TN 38116

Date: _____

Dear Mr. and Mrs. _____:

It has been brought to my attention that your child, _____, has missed _____ days during this school year. Please be advised that this number exceeds the designated limit (_____ days) of absences set forth in Board of Education Policy #_____.

According to this policy, a retention review will take place to determine whether your child should be promoted to the next grade.

Please call the Counseling Office at _____ to arrange for a conference to discuss your child's absences. Failure to do so may result in a five-day legal notice being sent to you. It is imperative that we take immediate action to avoid any future absences. Please bring any medical or other pertinent documentation with you to the scheduled conference.

Thank you for your understanding and consideration in this matter.

Sincerely yours,

_____
Barbara DiPentino
Counselor

Notice of Absences Approaching Limit, Grades 7–12

Some states have established minimum rules for attendance and have charged local school districts with adopting their own policies, thus permitting them to go beyond minimums if necessary. Many districts have done just that, some to the point of instituting a regulation that stipulates that after a certain number of absences, approved or unapproved, a student can be dropped from a course. These districts have found that this single and rather extreme measure has dramatically improved class attendance. Here is a form appropriate for the secondary level. Note the cc: to the counselor as well as the inclusion of the word "us" in the final sentence.

■　　　■　　　■

Date: _____

To the Parents of: _____
Address:

Dear Parents:

This is to inform you that your child has been absent and/or late a significant number of times this year. School policy regarding attendance reads as follows:

> In order to receive credit for a course, a student's absence must be less than 20 days for a full-year course, 10 days for a semester course, 5 days for a quarter course, and 3 days for a summer school course. Three incidents of unexcused tardiness shall equal one unexcused absence.

Your child's attendance record indicates _____ days absent and _____ days late. As you can see, your son/daughter is rather close to the maximum number of days allowable for the following course(s):

Should you have any questions about the above information, do not hesitate to contact us.

Sincerely,

_____
Esther A. Maddox
Assistant Principal

cc: Principal
　　Counselor

Midpoint Attendance Notice

At the high-school level, the attendance situation can become more focused as school officials zero in on particular courses. Several states mandate that Boards of Education adopt very specific attendance policies. Here the classroom teacher is required to send a midpoint warning notice—a notice that can also send a signal to the counselor to become involved, if he or she hasn't already done so.

■   ■   ■

MIDPOINT ATTENDANCE NOTICE

Student: Grade:

Course: Date:

Dear Parent/Guardian:

Please be advised that your child, _____, has to date been absent _____ times and/or tardy _____ times from _____ class. This midpoint notice is not intended to question the validity of the absences, but only to inform you of the fact that they have occurred. As you are undoubtedly aware, success in school is often related to attendance.

The school has an obligation to record and then report to parents the attendance record of their child as well as to inform parents of various school policies. Please review the enclosed Minimum Attendance Policy adopted by our Board of Education.

If you have any questions, feel free to contact your child's grade level administrator, _____.

Sincerely,

_____
Teacher

cc: White—Parent
    Canary—Assistant Principal
    Pink—Counselor
    Green—Attendance Office

Drop Due to Absences Notice

Sometimes the limit of absences is reached.

■   ■   ■

Date: _____

Dear Parent/Guardian:

A careful review of your child _____'s attendance record has been conducted, and it is noted that he/she has reached the limit of absences in the following course(s):

_____

Your child was dropped from the course(s) and will receive no credit for participation. You might want to contact your child's counselor to determine how this action will affect promotion or graduation.

It appears that strict adherence to the Board of Education's Attendance Policy will determine your child's future status in his or her remaining classes. We look to you for your support concerning this matter.

If you have any further questions or concerns, don't hesitate to contact me.

Sincerely,

_____
Barbara Fletcher
Assistant Principal

cc: Principal
    Counselor
    Teacher
    Attendance

Another Attendance Issue: Cutting

Counselors have always been involved with class cutters, but it's the chronic ones who most concern counselors. Cutting classes can be symptomatic of other serious problems, some of which may be family-related. If there's no caring at home, your counselee may wonder why he should care in school. The actual cutting of a class can also become a power play—some students delight in seeing how much they can get away with.

In your attempt to solve the cutting situation, you might uncover—and have to deal with—the underlying cause(s).

■   ■   ■

Sample Cutting Policy

The following excerpt is from a school's student/parent handbook. Note that the stated policy is clear and to the point.

Students are expected to be in attendance, including in their respected classes, on all days that school is in session.

Class Cutting

1. First class cut: One office-assigned detention issued and parents notified.
2. Second cut: Two office-assigned detentions issued and parents notified.
3. Third cut and every cut thereafter: In-school suspension.

A zero will be given for any class work missed as a result of class cutting. Students who cut more than one class in a single day will be considered truant and assigned an in-school suspension.

Addressing Tardiness

If the school environment is lax, the lecture can be half over before the last student wanders in. In a very strict environment, teachers stand in doorways, stopwatches in hand. And in many schools, being late for one teacher is not nearly as serious as being late for another.

To attack the thorny problem of tardiness, the very first step to take is to define the term so that everyone, including the counselor, has a common base from which to work. An absolute must for any school that is serious about curtailing both tardiness and cutting is the annual publication of a student handbook that clearly spells out all regulations—and the consequences for not adhering to them. It makes good sense for you to continually underscore the use of this publication with your families.

■   ■   ■

Sample Tardiness Policy

Here is an excerpt from one student/parent handbook.

■   ■   ■

Students are expected to be present on all days that school is in session. The Hollyrock Board of Education permits absences from school for the following reasons *only:*

Personal illness
Religious holidays
Death in the family
Court appearances
School-sanctioned activities

It can be disconcerting to both teacher and students when an individual student enters a classroom late. It is imperative that students arrive at class on time. Consequently, three incidents of unexcused tardiness will equal one unexcused absence. Tardiness will be excused only for those reasons approved for excused absence.

Transfer Notice for Teachers

_____
(Date)

From: Counseling Department

To: All Affected Teachers

The following student has transferred _____ out of your class/_____ out of our school.

Name: _____   Student #: _____

Grade: _____   Home Address: _____

_____

Transfer Date: _____

Transferred to: Teacher _____   Room # _____

Transferred to: School _____   Location _____

Transfer Between Classes: Records Update

This form is used when students transfer from one class to another within a marking period, so that the receiving teacher has the proper information for assigning a grade. It is most commonly used in changing level of instruction.

■   ■   ■

GILMORE J. FISHER JUNIOR HIGH SCHOOL
LOWER FERRY ROAD
TRENTON, NJ 08618

Student Name: _____

Date of Transfer: _____

Name of Sending Teacher: _____

Subject: _____ Class Level: _____

Test Grades to Date: _____
_____

Quiz Grades to Date: _____

Other Grades: _____

Days Absent: _____
_____

Proficiency Information: _____
_____
_____

If you have the information below, please complete.

Student's Address: _____

Telephone: _____

Parent's Name: _____

Request for Transfer Records

COUNSELING DEPARTMENT
WORTH MIDDLE SCHOOL
NILES, FLORIDA

Date: _____

To Whom It May Concern:

_____ recently enrolled in our school on the following
date: _____.

In order to provide an optimum teaching and learning situation, we would appreciate
your forwarding to this office as soon as possible all available data that you might
have on this student with regard to test scores, health records, and any other information that could be useful for appropriate subject-area placement.

Thank you for your kind attention.

Sincerely yours,

_____
Counselor

Attention Counseling Department:

I, the undersigned, hereby authorize the release of all school records of my son/
daughter _____ to the receiving school,
_____.

_____
(Parent/Guardian)

_____
(Date)

Letter for Sending Records

This form can be used by the sending school to ensure that records have been received.

■   ■   ■

_____

(Date)

To _____:

As requested, enclosed are the records of our former student,

_____, who resided at _____

_____.

Please acknowledge the receipt of these records by completing the bottom portion of this letter and returning it to us at your earliest convenience. Feel free to contact me at _____ if you have questions regarding the placement of
　　　　　(telephone)
this student.

Thank you for your consideration.

Very truly yours,

_____

Counselor

- -

To: _____

We at _____ have received the records of _____. We do/do not have further questions at this time.

Yours truly,

_____

Request for Detailed School Report

Some requests for school records involve more than just sending a transcript.

■   ■   ■

THE CADMAN SCHOOL

Joan R. Wilson
Director of Admissions

REQUEST FOR SCHOOL REPORT

To be signed by the parent/guardian and completed by the principal, headmaster, or counselor.

_____ is an applicant to The Cadman School.
                    (Name of student)

I hereby authorize and request _____
                                          (Current school)
to forward the following directly to Cadman:

1. Complete transcript of grades, including the most recent marking period
2. Results of standardized and/or individual testing
3. Personal confidential recommendation listed on the reverse

_____ Name of parent/guardian
        (Please type/print)

_____ Signature

_____ Date submitted to current school

(Reverse Side of Request for Detailed School Report)

ADMINISTRATIVE RECOMMENDATION

The student named below is an applicant to The Cadman School. We would appreciate your candid assessment of the student (the assessment will remain confidential), and we thank you for your assistance.

Joan R. Wilson
Director of Admissions

_____
(Name of applicant)

Please check the appropriate descriptor for each characteristic.

	POOR	FAIR	GOOD	SUPERIOR
Academic potential				
Academic performance				
Honesty/Integrity				
Leadership				
Cooperation with adults				
Relations with peers				
Extracurricular interests/ abilities (please list)				
OVERALL EVALUATION AS A STUDENT				
OVERALL EVALUATION AS A PERSON				

Has the applicant ever been involved in a serious infraction of school rules?

Are there any special circumstances, strengths, or problems (emotional, psychological, or other) of which we should be aware?

Additional comments?

Name _____   Institution _____

Signature _____   Address _____

Title _____   _____

Date _____   Telephone _____

III. Counseling for the Future _____

The blueprint for counseling a student extends beyond twelfth grade: We must counsel for the future. There is a great deal to communicate to young people about postsecondary preparation, so counselors must start working with their counselees early (by the seventh grade, if possible) to ready them suitably for life after high school. Early intervention is the key.

All students need advance help and encouragement with scholastic matters, but it is especially important for those from low-income groups, where the difficulties are obviously much greater. Our nation continues to have a serious problem: Students are not aware that they need to enroll in the "right" courses, depending on their academic plans, in eighth or ninth grade. A middle or junior high school counselor can play a vital role in giving counselees a good start.

It seems obvious that the proper counseling of a student involves knowing not only where the youngster is coming from, but also what he is going toward. Essentially, counselors are directly involved in the maturation process. Thus, counselors need enough time with each student to jointly develop probable plans early on and to help the student work through them to completion. By the time a youngster has finished his high school career, he should be well on the road to success in his postsecondary life.

11. POSTSECONDARY PLANNING

Students, particularly seniors in high school, are often concerned with the question, "What will I do when I get out?" A key objective of any counseling program is for you and your counselee to work with postsecondary issues well before the twelfth year.

A major component of postsecondary planning is, of course, college admission; but not everybody goes—nor should they go—to college. Some kids just aren't into books; they're into something else. Some want to be employed; others want to "do their thing," with or without a paycheck. Still others want a year or two of specialized training before they move on to the world of work. While millions head to college in late summer, millions more head to work, the military, apprenticeships, or proprietary schools.

Career Counseling for All Students

Career counseling is *everyone's* job—it should not be left solely to a "career specialist." As you help your counselees, it is vital that you realize that in today's world everybody should participate; career education needs support from faculty, parents, and various segments of the community, including people from the professions, labor, and industry.

It is with career counseling in particular that you can make a definite mark on your students' lifelong development. In delivering career counseling services, keep the following guidelines in mind:

- Career counseling should occupy an important place in a school's guidance and counseling program.
- Career counseling should be for *all* students.
- Career planning is a lifelong process; therefore, any school program should be developmental from grades K through 12.

Letter to Parents About Career Planning Program (CPP)

Date: _____

Dear Parents:

Your youngster is about to share in a career and educational planning experience in school. On _____, all eighth-grade students will have the opportunity to participate in the American College Testing Corporation's *Career Planning Program (CPP)*.

The CPP consists of a series of questionnaires and tests that will provide a foundation for your youngster's continuing career exploration activities. More specifically, CPP results supply students with knowledge about their interests, past experiences, and abilities and help them relate this information to careers and job families in the world of work.

As a parent, your role in this process is vital. Parents have been found to be the single-most important influence on a student's career decision. Consequently, you can influence the *quality* of the decision-making process by your support *and* involvement.

Here are several ways in which you can help:

1. Be aware that many students feel lost and confused about planning for the future, but it is beneficial to begin talking with your son or daughter about his or her plans for after high school right now. Naturally, these plans will be modified many times, but it is important to gradually elicit his/her feelings and desires.

2. Encourage your youngster to invest his or her best thinking in the CPP. Remind your youngster that the findings can be utilized as a stepping-stone toward the eventual satisfactory realization of certain career goals and objectives.

3. As counselors, we will be discussing CPP results with our counselees once profiles have been received. You, too, are encouraged to review profile results with your son or daughter.

We thank you for your past cooperation and look forward to your future involvement as we work together to assist our young people in making intelligent and meaningful plans for the future.

Sincerely,

Barry Watson
Anita Fleming
Counselors

Résumé Tips for Students

DEVELOPING THAT JOB RÉSUMÉ

Dear Student:

You may want to give some thought to developing a job résumé. The importance of doing so should be especially obvious to those students who plan to enter the work force upon graduation from high school. In any case, developing a well-organized and comprehensive résumé should benefit everyone: It will help you see who you are and what you can do from a different perspective. Here are some of the major components:

— Personal description: name, address, phone number, date of birth, social security number

— Education: secondary school attended, last grade completed, subjects you concentrated on and enjoyed, extracurricular participation, other education-related experiences

— Previous jobs held: when, where, doing what

— Reference sources: supervisors in any previous jobs, teachers, counselors

— Special skills, e.g., typing, driving a tractor, managing your own small business, word processing, computer usage, graphic design

— Special interests or career goals, e.g., animals, communication, helping professions, automobiles

— Miscellaneous, e.g., driver's license, access to an automobile

— Other characteristics that are unique about you

Interview Tips for Students

EAST BRUNSWICK HIGH SCHOOL
COLLEGE & CAREER CENTER

INTERVIEW TIPS
"First Impressions Are Lasting"

Dear Job Seeker:

The above slogan is so true, especially where a job interview is concerned. If you are looking for a job, you should know that what you do and say during the first ten seconds of the job interview may determine whether you are hired. If the interviewer's first impression of your attitude, personality, or appearance is negative, you run the risk of being eliminated from further consideration for the job.

Keeping the following suggestions in mind could result in a successful interview and, in turn, the desired position.

1. MAKE A GOOD APPEARANCE: Dress properly, display good posture, and present a pleasant manner. Even though public schools no longer have strict dress codes, the business world *does* pay close attention to clothing and grooming.

2. Be prepared by having a pen and/or pencil available to complete any forms.

3. Do not chew gum.

4. If possible, locate in advance the office in which the interview will be conducted.

5. On the day of the interview, allow sufficient reporting time in case you are unexpectedly delayed in arriving at your destination.

6. Arrive for the interview about ten minutes ahead of schedule.

7. Do not bring anyone to the interview with you.

8. THINK AHEAD: Anticipate some of the questions you might be asked—

   - your health
   - your grades in school
   - your social security number
   - history of past employment
   - hobbies
   - your use of leisure time
   - school activities
   - community activities

- your knowledge of the job you are seeking
- your knowledge of the firm

NOTE: You are being referred to an employer for a job interview by the College & Career Center. *Please* report back to us on the following school day as to the results of the interview, whether positive or negative. Whether we recommend you for future job interviews depends on your fulfilling this simple responsibility.

Good luck!

Robert E. Sullivan
Counselor

Job Information Form

FROM THE COLLEGE & CAREER CENTER

Here's the Job Information You Requested

EMPLOYER: _____   PHONE: _____

ADDRESS: _____   CONTACT: _____

           _____

JOB TITLE: _____   PAY: _____

HOURS: _____

NOTE: If you are under 18 years of age, you will need working papers. The first step is to have your new employer complete *Promise of Employment* papers. These forms are available in the College & Career Center. BE SURE TO REPORT THE RESULTS OF YOUR JOB SEARCH TO US AS SOON AS POSSIBLE.

Good Luck!

_____
Robert E. Sullivan
Counselor

Letter to New Student Employees

EAST BRUNSWICK HIGH SCHOOL
COLLEGE & CAREER CENTER

Employee Responsibilities

Dear Employee:

Congratulations on your new job!

You have been placed in this job through the College & Career Center's placement service. As a result, you assume a responsibility not only for yourself, but also for your school. You should make every effort to be an efficient and loyal employee, while at the same time maintaining a satisfactory school record. Your academic progress will be checked each marking period. Should it appear that you are experiencing scholastic difficulty, you will be invited to the Center for a conference.

I will ask your employer to periodically complete a brief evaluation form, which will enable me to track your progress. Make certain that your employer is notified immediately any time you cannot report to work. Also, feel free to see me if you have any job-related concerns, i.e., relationships with other employees or your employer, questions relative to whether you should leave a job, etc. Incidentally, if you intend to leave a job, please see me *prior* to giving notice.

You will need working papers if you are less than eighteen years of age.

Remember: Every job well done is a recommendation for another job.

Good luck!

Robert E. Sullivan
Counselor

Student Employee Evaluation Form

A job *is* a learning experience, and career counselors *do* counsel young people; therefore, the following evaluative instrument can be most useful in the counseling process.

■   ■   ■

EAST BRUNSWICK HIGH SCHOOL
COLLEGE & CAREER CENTER

(Date)

Dear Employer:

Would you please take a moment to complete this brief work evaluation form? Thank you.

Student Name: _____ Employer: _____

WORK EVALUATION (Please check the appropriate column.)

QUALITIES	SUPERIOR	ABOVE AVERAGE	AVERAGE	BELOW AVERAGE	POOR
Interest in Work					
Job Performance					
Attendance					
Appearance					

REMARKS: _____

_____

_____

_____   _____
Signature of Evaluator   Evaluator's Position

Please return the completed form to: Robert E. Sullivan, College & Career Center, East Brunswick High School, East Brunwick, NJ 08816

Free Materials Request

Here is a time-saving note to outside agencies requesting free career/educational materials.

■   ■   ■

COLLEGE & CAREER CENTER
EAST BRUNSWICK HIGH SCHOOL

Dear Sir/Madam:

Please send two copies of any available career/educational materials that might be suitable for use by high school students and/or counselors.

Thank you for your cooperation.

Sincerely,

Robert E. Sullivan, Counselor
College & Career Center
East Brunswick High School
East Brunswick, NJ 08816

Letter to New Graduates

June 25, 19_____

Dear 19_____ Graduate:

Please accept a complimentary copy of our publication entitled, *That Job Search.* We produced it in order to assist you in your search for an appropriate part-time or full-time job. This booklet should enable you to have a competitive edge over other individuals in the job market.

We hope that those who plan on immediate employment will get off to a more productive start through the use of this material. Those graduates who plan to continue education at a college or proprietary school might find the booklet helpful in securing summer employment.

Remember—the staff at the Career Center is also here to help graduates. We may be able to assist you as you enter this new stage in your life.

Best wishes for future success!

Sincerely,

_____

Brad Epstein
Career Counselor

Career Program Invitation to Parents

Career Day/Career Night programs are really the exception rather than the rule in secondary schools. Unfortunately, this worthwhile endeavor tends to get lost in the push to present an assortment of more glamorous college planning programs. Too bad! Not only can such an effort broaden a total counseling program, it can also greatly enhance community relations.

■   ■   ■

Date: _____

Dear Parents:

On Wednesday, March 24, at 7:30 P.M., the Counseling Department will hold a Career Exploration program throughout the high school.

You and your child will have an unusual opportunity to hear and speak with many members of our professional and business community with regard to various occupations, including entry-level requirements and general expectations.

We believe that this kind of endeavor will lead to more informed choices of careers by our students.

Additional information will follow. We look forward to having you with us on the evening of March 24.

Sincerely,

_____

Judith M. Bartley
Director of Counseling

Career Program Invitation to Speakers

Date: _____

Dear _____ :

You are invited to participate in a Career Exploration program to be held on Wednesday, March 24, at 7:30 P.M., here at Woodrow Wilson High School.

We are extending this invitation to business and professional leaders to meet with our students and their parents to orient them toward various occupations, including an explanation of entry-level requirements, the pluses and minuses of particular jobs, and, most importantly, your own personal insights into your occupation. As you know, there is nothing like hearing it from the source.

Such an affair should lead to more informed career choices by our students.

We are confident that our students and their parents will enjoy listening to you. Similarly, you should find the experience to be a rewarding one. Can we count on you to join us for the evening? Please notify us of your intentions by March 15 at (000) 555-1212.

Sincerely,

_____
Judith M. Bartley
Director of Counseling

September Senior Questionnaire

In this case, with the cooperation of the Physical Education Department, counselors meet with seniors in September and ask them to complete a brief questionnaire. The student's commitment in writing can translate into moving more quickly on any issue that needs attention. Also, counselors can readily see how much progress has been made by their counselees in the postsecondary educational planning process.

■   ■   ■

MADISON HIGH SCHOOL
MADISON, NEW JERSEY 07940

FALL QUERY FOR SENIORS

September 19_____

STUDENT: _____ COUNSELOR: _____ P.E. Period _____

1. After high school I plan to: (Circle *one* choice below.)
   A. Attend a four-year college
   B. Attend a two-year college
   C. Attend a trade, technical, or business school
   D. Enter one of the armed services
   E. Seek employment
   F. I am undecided

If you plan to attend college or a trade, technical, or business school, complete questions 2 through 9; if not, complete questions 8 through 10.

2. I have sent for the
   following applications: I have visited: I plan to apply to:

   _____   _____   _____

   _____   _____   _____

   _____   _____   _____

   _____   _____   _____

   _____   _____   _____

   _____   _____   _____

3. I have asked the following teachers for letters of recommendation:

   _____   _____

   _____   _____

(Senior Questionnaire, continued)

4. Have you prepared a list of your activities?   Yes _____   No _____

   If so, have you given it to your teachers?   Yes _____   No _____

   Do you have a copy in your personal folder?   Yes _____   No _____

5. I plan to apply: Early Decision _____   Early Action _____   Regular _____

6. Do you need help with your college essays?   Yes _____   No _____

7. I plan to attend college, but I have done little or nothing yet. (Circle statement if correct.)

8. When is the most convenient time for you to see your counselor?

   Before school _____   Elective periods _____   Study Hall _____   Other _____

9. Would your parents like a conference?   Yes _____   No _____

10. If you don't plan to continue your education after graduation, could you use some assistance in planning your future?   Yes _____   No _____

Graduating Senior Questionnaire

NAME: _____

Note that there are four sections listed below. In completing this form, please respond to the *one* section that relates to your post-high school plans. Return this form *personally* to your counselor at the time of your farewell interview. THIS FORM MUST BE COMPLETED AND RETURNED IN ORDER FOR YOU TO OBTAIN GRADUATION MATERIALS.

I. FULL-TIME EMPLOYMENT (NOTE: Do not complete this section if you have a summer job only.)

Do you have a promise of full-time employment?   Yes _____ No _____

If "Yes," what type of job will you have and with what company?

JOB: _____   COMPANY: _____

If "No," are you seeking full-time employment?   Yes _____ No _____

What kind of job are you looking for? _____

II. ARMED FORCES

Do you plan to enlist in a branch of the armed forces? Yes _____ No _____

If "Yes," which branch? _____

Approximate enlistment date: _____

III. TRADE, TECHNICAL, OR BUSINESS SCHOOL

Do you plan to attend one of the above-mentioned institutions?

Yes _____ No _____

If "Yes," what is the name and location of the institution? _____

_____

What type of program will you be pursuing? _____

IV. COLLEGE/UNIVERSITY

Final Grade Point Average: _____ Class Rank: _____

Highest SAT Scores: Verbal _____ Math _____

ACT Composite: _____

(Graduating Senior Questionnaire, continued)

Applications Sent to:

INSTITUTION   STATE   ZIP CODE   ACCEPTED   REJECTED   ATTENDING

_____

_____

_____

_____

NOTE: Please supply us with a stamped envelope addressed to the college of your choice so that we can mail a final transcript.

Would you be willing to accept telephone calls from future seniors who might have questions about the college you are attending?   Yes _____ No _____

_____   _____
Signature   Phone #

Farewell Senior Conference Notice

A special "farewell" interview for graduating seniors can be enhanced by including a "special" office pass.

■　　■　　■

FAREWELL CONFERENCE

HOMEROOM:

STUDENT:　　　　　　　　　　　　　　APPOINTMENT TIME:

Dear Senior:

Please report to the Counseling Office at the time indicated above. Bring the following with you:

　　1. The completed senior questionnaire distributed to you in English class.

　　2. If you will be registering at a college or university, a stamped envelope addressed to the college or university you will be attending.

RETURN TIME:　　　　　　　　　　_____
　　　　　　　　　　　　　　　　　　　COUNSELOR

12.   COLLEGE ADMISSIONS

Of all the things counselors do in working with their students, college counseling has got to be the most controversial. Counselors are either: spending too much time with this task or not enough; overly involved with recommending schools or not into it enough; too influential when it comes to kids taking the "right" courses for college or too passive. It's probably the most "damned if you do and damned if you don't" aspect of the total counseling role. And we have the added responsibility of trying to communicate effectively with a variety of higher education officials in addition to our "regulars"—students, parents, teachers, and colleagues.

Pre-college counseling *should not* be just for those who say they expect to go to college. Young people with good collegiate potential sometimes come from homes where interest in this alternative is minimal. Students who say "probably not" are the very ones who need support, encouragement, and concrete advice on how to further explore their options. The challenge is to work toward a systemwide developmental approach that renders greater consistency to the counseling of each student. Remember, college counseling is just one important facet of a department's total developmental program.

The sample letters, memos, and forms in this topic should help free you to do more supporting, encouraging, and advising.

College Admissions Time Line

A TIME LINE FOR COLLEGE ADMISSIONS

11th grade: FALL	Begin Research on Colleges and Universities
October	Take PSAT
11th grade: SPRING	Conduct Intensive Research
	First College Visitation Period
April/May	Take First SAT and/or ACT
June	Appropriate Time for Certain Achievement Tests
11th–12th grades: SUMMER	Send for Applications
	Second College Visitation Period
12th grade: FALL	Complete and Mail Applications
	Third College Visitation Period
October/November	Take Second SAT and/or ACT
12th grade: WINTER December– January	Appropriate Time for Remaining Achievements
January– February	Complete and Mail Financial Aid Forms
12th grade: SPRING March–April	Make Final Decisions

College Fair Seminar Request to College Reps

Student seminars can make a local or regional minicollege fair program more vital and purposeful. The objective is to give sophomores and/or juniors in-depth exposure to the college planning process. There is nothing like hearing the word from a variety of college representatives. Parents can be invited to participate, and relationships will be enhanced all the way around.

When college reps accept an invitation to represent their school at a mini-fair, they are asked to staff panels for two, forty-two minute periods. Reps are given a preference for topics listed, and panels are then balanced as to competitiveness of admission, large/small enrollment, and public/private orientation.

■   ■   ■

_____, 19_____

Dear _____:

We are pleased that you have agreed to represent your institution on _____, at our college fair program.

As part of the overall program, we will conduct a series of seminars to enhance our students' college planning skills. We would appreciate it if you would participate in the seminars, discussing one topic at two sessions.

Enclosed are two copies of the six topics. Please rank these topics in order of your preference for speaking, and return one copy to us ASAP. We will get back to you as to your assignment.

Again, welcome, and thank you for taking the time to participate. If you have any further questions or concerns, don't hesitate to telephone me.

Sincerely,

_____
Counselor

College Fair Seminar Descriptions

Date: _____

Dear Student:

As part of our forthcoming minicollege fair program, a series of seminars will be conducted from 12:30 P.M. to 2:00 P.M. You will have the opportunity to participate in *two* seminars. Please review the six topics listed below, and indicate two seminars that you are tentatively interested in attending. We need to obtain some idea of the number of sections that will be needed for each topic. Actual sign-ups will take place at a later date during lunch periods. *You need not sign your name.*

Check two (2) below:

_____ 1. *How the College Looks at the Candidate.* We'll have an inside examination of what admission offices are looking for in a candidate and how these same offices handle student applications.

_____ 2. *What College Catalogs Don't Tell You.* There is much more to the collegiate experience than what is contained in a college catalog. Let's view the whole scene and explore ways in which you can take a comprehensive look at a particular college or university.

_____ 3. *Special Needs/Problems of the Student Athlete.* The recruitment of high school athletes continues to be a high priority with colleges and universities. Young student athletes are often faced with difficult decisions—Who can help? What can be believed?

_____ 4. *Visiting the College Campus.* Getting out and onto the campus is critical. There is nothing like seeing the school firsthand and speaking with enrolled students. Learn how to make the most of the college visitation, including how to present your "best self" when interviewing.

_____ 5. *Preparing an Effective College Application.* No typos or misspellings, please! Applications do vary as to the difficulty of completion. Here's your chance to receive solid advice on how to submit a quality piece to the college of your choice.

_____ 6. *Grades Versus SATs: What's Really Important?* How much do test scores really count? What about the quality of course work? What about weighted rank? Come join in a discussion of the value of course grades and admission test scores.

College Fair Evaluation

Dear College Admission Counselor:

You have spent a full day and evening with us at Bradford High School. We were pleased that you were able to attend our minicollege fair. It was a most rewarding and profitable experience from our point of view. Would you please take a moment to complete this evaluation survey? Thank you.

Sincerely,

Richard Carlson, Chairman

Please Rate the Following Activities:

	Excellent	Good	Fair	Poor
Senior Panel				
Counselor Workshop				
Buffet Lunch				
Student Seminars				
Evening College Fair				

What one aspect of the program did you find most beneficial? Why?

What aspect(s) of the program would you modify? How and why?

Was there a missing element? If so, what was it?

Additional Comments:

Student Panel Agenda

Some secondary schools utilize recently "accepted" seniors as important resource personnel in the college planning process. You can staff a senior panel in May for juniors and/or visiting college representatives, or invite seniors back the following academic year at holiday time. The key to a successful presentation is to find warm, friendly, and articulate panelists who can project themselves well. *Don't* stack the panel with just "top" students. Find six or so that represent a cross section of colleges and universities, from highly to less competitive for admission, large to small, and public or private.

■   ■   ■

Student Panel Agenda

I.   Opening remarks by school counselor and introduction of student moderator

II.   Moderator introduction; panelists' introduction of themselves (minute-long statement)

III.   Discussion of the following questions by panelists:

1.   Generally speaking, what would you want to tell the college admission representatives/junior students about the admission process?

2.   What were the most enjoyable aspects of the admission process for you and why?

3.   What were the most difficult aspects for you and why? What might the colleges have done to make these aspects less difficult?

IV.   Question-and-Answer Period

V.   Closing*

*A great finale for the presentation: Participants do not reveal what schools they will be attending until the last moment. At that time, they rise in place, reach for sweatshirts placed directly in front of them, and spread them across their chests.

Invitation to Parent for Pre-College Counseling

Date: _____

Dear _____:

You and your child are invited to meet with _____,
your counselor, in a pre-college counseling session to be held here at the
Counseling Department.

This will be an excellent opportunity for you and the counselor to discuss
areas of mutual concern related to the college admission process.

The conference should last approximately forty minutes. Your appointment
has been set for _____ at _____.

We look forward to having you with us.

Sincerely,

_____

Herbert M. Wilson
Department Chairperson

Notice to Parent of Student No-Shows

Here is a proactive memo that alerts parents to activities missed by their youngsters.

■   ■   ■

CEDAR RIDGE HIGH SCHOOL
OLD BRIDGE, NEW JERSEY 08857

Date: _____

Dear Mr./Mrs. _____:

Group meetings to explain the college admission process, including specific application procedures, were recently held here in the Counseling Office. At each meeting, I oriented my students to all of our many available planning resources, such as the computer search program, VCR tapes, guidebooks, and college catalogs.

_____ was sent passes on three different occasions but
     (Student Name)
failed to appear or respond.

It is the Counseling Department's aim to help students and their families in the postsecondary education planning process. I will continue to try to meet with your youngster, but I would also welcome your assistance in making such a meeting a reality.

Sincerely,

_____
Counselor

Agenda for Parent's Program

PARENT'S SURVIVAL GUIDE
TO THE COLLEGE ADMISSION PROCESS
(A Two-Part Seminar)

SEMINAR I   7:30 P.M., Wednesday, March 19, 19_____

    Self-Assessment and College Selection
    Examining the Market
    Refining Your Options
    The Campus Visit and Interview

SEMINAR II   7:30 P.M., Wednesday, March 26, 19_____

    Completing the Application
    The Personal Essay
    Counselor/Teacher Involvement
    Financing the Venture
    Stress Factors That Affect the Collegebound

College Planning Ladder

THE COLLEGE PLANNING LADDER

Where are you on the College Planning Ladder? How can we help you get to the next step? Cross off any item that is completed or under way or that does not apply to you. Place a check mark next to the items with which you would like some assistance. Then share this ladder with your counselor so that he or she can give you a boost!

Handle timing and deadline problems.

Do additional in-depth research on selected schools.

Apply for financial aid.

Mail applications.

Adjust choices based on new senior grades/test scores.

Shape the personal essay.

Address the logistics of requesting transcripts and other forms.

Get teacher recommendations.

Apply for particular admission testing programs.

Complete the application.

Visit campuses and/or set up interviews.

Settle on a final list of schools.

Arrange schools according to selectivity levels.

Procure applications and publications.

Develop a list of possible colleges.

Discuss intended major—or lack thereof.

Decide on the type of college.

Decide whether to go to college.

Examine possible career paths.

Plan to graduate from high school.

Coping with College Boards

Researchers at the Carnegie Foundation for the Advancement of Teaching estimate that there are "probably fewer than 50 colleges and universities in the United States today that can be considered highly selective, admitting less than half the students who apply." If we stretch this statistic a bit to include all of the "most," "highly +," and "highly" selective institutions categorized in the *Comparative Guide to American Colleges,* we arrive at about 100 schools, most of which rely heavily on standardized testing for their selection process. That leaves 2,900 others, one-third of which maintain open-door admission policies. Clearly, the overwhelming majority of collegiate institutions in America base their decision on quality of course work pursued, grades received, required essays, and an assortment of nonacademic factors. Nevertheless, standardized testing is a persistent reality with which we must deal.

■   ■   ■

College Admission Testing Information: PSAT, SAT, and ACH

The following information works well as a handout for students and parents.

■   ■   ■

COLLEGE ADMISSION TESTING PROGRAMS IN A NUTSHELL

The following standardized tests are administered by the Educational Testing Service (ETS) for the College Entrance Examination Board (CEEB). They are sometimes referred to as the "college boards."

Preliminary Scholastic Aptitude Test (PSAT)

This test is an abbreviated version of the Scholastic Aptitude Test (SAT). It has two sections: verbal and mathematics. The PSAT is offered only in October, and it is primarily for juniors. Scores are reported on a scale of 20–80. It is considered a practice test, and results are not reported to colleges unless a student specifically requests them to be.

The National Merit Scholarship Corporation uses PSAT results as an initial screening device for those juniors who wish to be considered for National Merit recognition. A selective index score is derived by doubling the PSAT verbal score and adding the mathematics score. The top one-half of one percent of the students in *each* state are designated as "semifinalists" in the competition. Those students who fall immediately below semifinalist status and who are in the top five percent of the students in each state are designated as "commended" students.

(College Admission Testing Information, continued)

Scholastic Aptitude Test (SAT)

The SAT is a three-hour achievement/aptitude test administered six times yearly. Scores on the two main sections (verbal and mathematics) are reported on a scale of 200–800. Subscores in reading and vocabulary are reported on a scale of 20–80. The score on the separate Test of Standard Written English (TSWE) is reported on a scale of 20–60+.

The SAT normally is taken by juniors in May or June of junior year and by seniors in November or December of senior year.

Achievement Tests (ACHs)

The Achievement Tests cover sixteen different subject-matter areas. All of the tests call for one hour of multiple-choice testing, except the English Composition with Essay, which consists of a twenty-minute essay and forty minutes of multiple-choice questions. Each test is designed to measure knowledge and the ability to apply this knowledge in one subject area. It is best to take an ACH as close as possible to the end of study in a subject-matter area, while the material is still fresh in one's mind.

The sixteen different tests fall into five curricular areas: English (English Composition, Literature), Foreign Languages (French, German, Modern Hebrew, Latin, Spanish, Italian), History and Social Studies (American History and European History), Mathematics (Math Level I, Math Level II, Math II Calculator), and Sciences (Biology, Chemistry, Physics).

Approximately 150 of the nation's 3,000 colleges and universities require one or more of these tests for admission or placement. Scores range from 200–800. The tests are administered five times yearly: November, December, January, May, and June.

Advanced Placement Tests (AP)

Many high schools offer a variety of Advanced Placement (AP) courses—college-level courses that are academically challenging and which prepare the student to take a final AP examination in May of the academic year. Students who earn high scores on one or more of these tests may place out of and/or receive credit for a particular course offered by the college of their choice. In short, a college may either exempt a student from a beginning-level course or offer him or her advanced standing, enabling the student to take fewer credits once on campus. Advanced standing in several courses can result in significant savings in tuition costs.

Common ACH Questions

OFTEN-ASKED ACH QUESTIONS

1. *What are the Achievement Tests (ACH)?*
   The Achievement Tests are part of the College Board's Admissions Testing Program (ATP). The series covers sixteen different subject-matter areas. All of the tests call for one hour of testing time, except the English Composition with Essay, which consists of a twenty-minute essay and forty minutes of multiple-choice questions. Approximately 155 of the nation's 3,000 colleges and universities require one or more of these tests for admission or placement.

2. *Do I need to take these tests?*
   If you plan to apply to one of the more selective colleges in the country, the ACH *may* be required. As you can see in the above paragraph, most colleges and universities do not require them. While you might not have a definite college choice in mind, you probably have some idea as to the type and selectivity of the institutions to which you ultimately will apply.

3. *How do I know if the colleges of my choice require these tests?*
   The *College Handbook,* a publication of the College Board, gives a comprehensive description of college entrance test requirements. The brochures and catalogs of various institutions provide even better information about such testing requirements.

4. *What are the subject areas the tests cover?*
   The sixteen different tests fall into five curricular areas: English (English Composition, Literature), Foreign Languages (French, German, Modern Hebrew, Latin, Spanish, Italian), History and Social Studies (American History and European History), Mathematics (Math Level I, Math Level II, Math Level IIC), and Sciences (Biology, Chemistry, Physics).

5. *When are the tests given?*
   They are administered five times yearly: November, December, January, May, and June. Specific dates are listed in the *Registration Bulletin for the SAT and Achievement Tests* and in a special informative booklet, *Taking the Achievement Tests.* Both of these publications are official guides of the College Board and are available in the Counseling Office.

6. *When is the best time to take these tests?*
   It is best to take an ACH as close to the end of study in a subject-matter area as possible—while the material is still fresh in your mind. Please note that the English Composition with Essay, required by a few schools, is only administered in the month of December.

7. *How do I sign up?*
   Use the same application as for the SAT. The application is located in the center of the *Registration Bulletin for the SAT and Achievement Tests.* You

(Common ACH Questions, continued)

do not need to indicate which test(s) you will be taking. You can make this decision at the time of testing.

8. *How do I know which tests to take?*
   After you have determined that the college(s) of your choice requires the ACH, it is good practice to consult the catalogs of those institutions. College catalogs will provide you with the most reliable information as to what is required. Your teachers, as well as your counselor, can advise you regarding the level of success you might expect to achieve.

9. *How will colleges and universities use my test results?*
   College publications will generally provide this information in the section entitled, "Admission Requirements." Usually, if an institution will accept scores after January, the results are used for placement and/or credit, not selection purposes.

10. *What happens to my scores after I take the ACH?*
    Your scores are reported to those colleges and universities you designate on your test application. It is important to note, however, that as you request sets of scores, each computerized report lists all previous results, from the most current back to the first test taken in the ATP program.

ACT Information Sheet

THE AMERICAN COLLEGE TESTING PROGRAM

The American College Testing Program is an independent, nonprofit educational service organization. The ACT Assessment Program is taken by more than one million collegebound students each year.

The ACT has four sections that measure academic achievement: English, reading (social studies/sciences/arts/literature), mathematics, and science reasoning. Each section is scored separately, and a composite score is then determined. The composite score is the most commonly reported index in the program.

After nearly thirty years of use, the ACT underwent a substantial face-lifting in 1989. The enhancements introduced by the Iowa-based corporation were the most comprehensive to date.

Here is a convenient guide that compares features of the current SAT and the new ACT. It can provide you with the opportunity to make a comparison and then to select the option that will best support your application.

CONTENT COMPARISON OF THE ACT AND SAT

	ACT Assessment	*Scholastic Aptitude Test*
Purpose:	Measures classroom achievement in four broad content areas as well as the ability to reason and to apply problem-solving skills	Measures academic aptitude in terms of verbal and mathematical reasonsing and the ability to recognize standard written English

Content:		Verbal
		    Antonyms
		    Analogies
		    Sentence completion

	Reading test
	    Arts/literature
	    Social studies/sciences
		Reading comprehension in social,
		    political, scientific, artistic,
		    philosophical, and literary areas

	English test
	    Usage/mechanics
	    Rhetorical skills
		Standard written English
		    Punctuation
		    Grammar
		    Sentence structure
		    Diction and style

	Mathematics test
	    Pre-algebra
	    Elementary algebra
	    Intermediate algebra
	    Coordinate geometry
	    Plane geometry
	    Trigonometry
	Science reasoning test
		Mathematics
		    Arithmetic
		    Algebra
		    Geometry
		    Other topics (logic and operations)

Topics for a Seminar on Athletics

SEMINAR ON ATHLETICS

PLANNING TO GET THERE

Topic I: SELECTING THAT COLLEGE

- Athletics as a Factor in Selecting a College
- Special Admissions Considerations for Athletes
- What the Athlete Should Look for in a College
- The Two-Year College Approach

Topic II: COLLEGE RECRUITERS: HOW TO WORK WITH THEM

- The Student as an *Active* Participant in the Recruiting Game
- Official Recruiting Regulations
- What to Look for in a Recruiter's Sales Pitch
- Important Questions to Ask Recruiters

Topic III: FINANCING A COLLEGE EDUCATION

- The Pros and Cons of Athletic Scholarships
- Who Receives Scholarship Offers
- How to Promote an Offer
- Special Considerations in Awarding Aid to Athletes

WINNING IN COLLEGE

Topic IV: MAINTAINING ELIGIBILITY

- Why Have Eligibility Rules?
- NCAA and NAIA Eligibility Rules
- Penalties for Violating Regulations
- Staying on Top of Academic Requirements
- Academic Standing: From Dean's List to Disqualification
- The Athlete's Support System

Topic V: STUDYING AND COPING SKILLS

- Coping with the "Dumb Jock" Image
- Asserting Yourself as a "Student"
- Time Management: *The* Critical Skill for the Student Athlete
- Building Learning Skills for College
- How to Deal with Poor Performance: Will Anyone Notice?

Invitation to Speak on Student Athlete Panel

Date: _____

Dear _____ :

On _____, _____, we will hold a minicollege fair for our students. As part of the overall program, we will conduct a series of seminars to enhance our students' college planning skills. One of the seminars is designed to address the special needs and problems of the student athlete, as experienced at both the pre-college and college levels:

> *Special Needs/Problems of the Student Athlete.* The recruitment of high school athletes continues to be a high priority with colleges and universities. Young student athletes are often faced with difficult decisions—Who can help? What can be believed?

There will be two, forty-two minute presentations between the hours of 12:30 P.M. and 2:00 P.M. We would then like to present the same topic to available high school coaches and counselors from 2:15 P.M. to 3:15 P.M.

You and two other college coaches have been recommended as individuals who are most qualified to present this kind of material. Therefore, we would be pleased if you would consent to join us on the afternoon of _____. Can you be here? Please notify us by _____.

Thank you for your consideration.

_____
Chairman, Counseling Department

_____
Director of Athletics

Information for Student Athlete Panel Speakers

_____, 19_____

Dear _____:

We are pleased that you have agreed to join us on _____, _____, for the sports portion of our minicollege fair program. Two other panelists will be with you on this occasion.

Could you please meet with me in the counseling office at 12:00 noon on that day to discuss the format of the panel?

We will be offering two sessions of "Special Problems/Needs of the Student Athlete," beginning at 12:30 P.M.; each will last forty-two minutes.

A similar presentation of this seminar will take place at 2:15 P.M. for high school coaches and counselors. This particular session should permit more time to explore the issues in depth.

Enclosed are two copies of the five major issues. Please rank these topics in order of your preference for speaking, and return one copy to us ASAP. We will get back to you as to your assignment.

Again, welcome, and thank you for taking the time to participate. If you have any further questions or concerns, don't hesitate to telephone me.

Sincerely,

_____
Counselor

cc: Director of Athletics

Invitation to Attend Athletics Seminar

Here is an invitation to your high school coaches, counselors, and other athletically involved personnel:

■   ■   ■

_____, 19_____

Dear _____:

We would like to invite you to attend a seminar on "Special Problems/Needs of the Student Athlete."

This unusual program should be a good opportunity for you to strengthen the advisory skills you use with your athletes concerning college planning, especially as this planning relates to actual sports participation on the collegiate level.

The program will be held on _____, _____, at 2:15 P.M. in the Lecture Hall.

Presenters will include:

We look forward to having you with us on the afternoon of _____.

Sincerely,

_____

Athletic Director

_____

Counselor

Checklist for the Athlete

CHECKLIST FOR THE ATHLETE

1. What will be my total cost per year *over* the scholarship?

2. What are the prevailing campus attitudes toward various minorities, ethnic groups, and religious affiliations?

3. Are special programs in academic counseling and/or tutoring available?

4. Do I get a comfortable feeling when I visit the campus?

5. How does the school stand academically?

6. What are the course requirements of the academic department in which I am interested? What time demands will be placed on me?

7. How and where will I fit into the athletic program: starter? specialist?

8. Do they have plans to "red shirt" me?

9. I might want to play both fall and spring sports. If I am being considered primarily for a fall sport, will there be spring ball? What *is* the athletic department's attitude toward two-sport athletes?

10. How stable is the coaching staff in terms of employment?

11. Am I really being *offered* a scholarship, or are we just at the talking stage?

12. How are the players generally treated?

13. Can I meet the coaching staff?

Counselor's College Rep Interview Sheet

This handy form can be used to secure data from a visiting college representative.

■   ■   ■

COLLEGE REP INTERVIEW SHEET

Name of Institution: _____

Date of Visit: _____

Representative's Name: _____

Director of Admissions: _____

Telephone: _____

Unusual Majors: _____

_____

Updated Costs: _____

Academic Scholarships? _____

On/Off-Campus Employment Opportunities? _____

Percentage of Students on Financial Aid: _____

Field Experience, Internships, and Special Programs: _____

_____

Housing Situation: _____

Separate Admission Criteria for Different Areas? _____

_____

Placement Trends: _____

_____

SAT/ACT Profile? _____

Class Rank/GPA Profile? _____

Comments:

Pass to Meet with College Rep

STUDENT PASS

TO: _____

FROM: Counseling Department

RE: Educational and Career Information Program

If convenient, would you please release the following student to the Counseling Office to hear a special presentation?

STUDENT: _____   DATE: _____

PERIOD: _____   INSTITUTION: _____

TEACHER'S SIGNATURE: _____   TIME LEFT: _____

COUNSELOR'S SIGNATURE: _____   RETURN TIME: _____

COMMENTS:

Reverse side:

NOTE TO STUDENT:

In order to participate in a meaningful dialogue at this presentation, you *must* research the following basic information:

1. Type and size of school? _____
    (specialized/arts & sciences, coed/single sex, public/private)

2. Location, including distance from home in miles? _____

    _____

3. Visiting school's mean SAT scores?   V _____   M _____

    Your scores?   V _____   M _____

4. Do you have a tentative or definite major in mind? If yes, what is it?

    _____

    Does this school have it? _____

Sample Inquiry Paragraphs

SAMPLE INQUIRY PARAGRAPHS

Pick a paragraph or combination of paragraphs that might meet your needs:

Paragraph A—General Information Request Letter
Paragraph B—Campus Visitation Letter
Paragraph C—Financial Aid Letter

■   ■   ■

Your Name
Home Address
Date

Office of Undergraduate Admissions
Name of Institution
Address

To Whom It May Concern:

I plan to enroll in college with the term beginning _____.
(month & year)

A. Please send me an application, catalog, and any additional information that I might need. I am considering _____ as a possible major.

B. I would like to visit your campus and meet with an admission counselor. Since I am considering majoring in _____, would it be possible to meet with someone from that department? Please advise me of a convenient date and time for my visit.

C. My family and I would like to further investigate college costs and potential sources of financial aid. Please send us updated price information and specifics concerning how, when, and where to apply for financial aid.

Thank you for your consideration.

Sincerely,

Inquiry—Postcard Format

Here is another inquiry piece. Gone are the days when admission officers determined their applicants' admissibility by scrutinizing request letters for errors in spelling and grammar. Therefore, students should feel free to submit a *plain* postcard in making their requests. Care should be taken to complete the cards neatly, because these handy little cards have ended up in admission folders. Students should mention their prospective major, if they know it, since schools often publish special departmental brochures. Students should be up front as to their need for financial assistance as well. Note the unusual last paragraph.

■　　　■　　　■

Dear Admission Officer:

I am interested in applying to your school for admission in September 199____. Please send me an application, catalog, financial aid form, and any additional information that I might need. I am tentatively interested in majoring in _____.

Also, please inform me whether one of your representatives will be visiting this area in the near future, since I would be interested in speaking with him or her.

Sincerely,

_____
Robert S. Jordan
111 Sunset Avenue
West Wendor, NJ 09999

Learning Disability Support Services Inquiry

Since support services for the learning-disabled vary considerably from institution to institution, it is wise for the candidate to write directly to each college or university for the specifics of their program.

■   ■   ■

Student's Street Address

City, State, Zip

Date

Name of Director or Dean
Office of Undergraduate Admissions
Name of College or University
City, State, Zip

Dear _____:

I have a learning disability and am completing my senior year at Madison High School. After I graduate in June, I plan to attend college.

Would you please send me information on the support services your school offers to its learning-disabled students? I would also appreciate receiving an application, catalog, and any additional information that I might need.

Thank you for your consideration.

Sincerely,

Name of Student

Special Concerns of Physically Handicapped Students

Webster defines the word *access* as "to get at." The word *accessible* is defined as "capable of being reached." The physically handicapped are forever trying to "reach" the classroom to "get at" knowledge.

No one knows better than the disabled person that the word "accessible" can mean different things to different schools. For example, on one campus, all buildings might be barrier-free; while on another campus, the administration might have to move an entire class to accommodate a single disabled student. Unfortunately, at some colleges and universities the admission interview might have to be moved because the candidate is unable to access the admissions office. Without a doubt, students with physical impairments provide a real challenge to all educational institutions at all educational levels.

The overriding concern of those who work to help the physically disabled achieve an education should be the removal of physical *and* attitudinal barriers. Transitional movement on the educational ladder needs to be as smooth as possible, so that the student can continue to successfully compete in each subsequent academic environment. In your capacity as a school counselor, you can play a decisive role.

■   ■   ■

Accessibility Checklist for Handicapped Students

Baker's Dozen of Things to Look for When Visiting That Educational Institution

1. Accessibility to key buildings
2. Properly graded ramps
3. Curb cuts
4. Automatic doors
5. Handicapped stalls, with appropriately placed grab bars, in restrooms
6. Elevators with control buttons at the proper level
7. Low telephones
8. Low drinking fountains
9. Handicapped parking spaces in strategic areas
10. Roll-in shower facilities/low sinks
11. Low closet rods
12. Other innovative housing arrangements
13. Special campus transportation systems

How to Judge a College at Its Worst

HOW TO JUDGE A COLLEGE AT ITS WORST
A Whimsical Guide with a Serious Side

In their literature or on their guided tour, colleges usually manage to show themselves "at their best." But during your four years there, you'll see your campus at its worst, too. Would you like a preview of coming attractions?

1. Have a meal in the student cafeteria on a Sunday evening.
2. Walk through the dormitories and fraternities at midnight during a party weekend.
3. Read the school paper the week before student government elections.
4. Mingle with the crowd during a postgame party on Homecoming Weekend.
5. Ask a freshman to tell you the name of the poorest section leader for a required freshman course. Attend his/her 8:00 A.M. Monday section, sitting in the last row in a broken chair, wearing pajamas under snowy clothes and wet socks.
6. Under the same circumstances, sit in a class that is taking a one-hour essay test. Take it yourself.
7. In a freezing rain, try to park your car near a main classroom building two minutes before class.
8. Ask a freshman how many classes are taught by graduate assistants or by someone other than the name printed in the catalog. Or, count in the catalog the number of "graduate fellowships" awarded, and assume that each fellow teaches two freshman classes.
9. Stop by the student newspaper office and ask to see (or buy) a copy of the student-written handbook of faculty ratings.
10. Ask a custodian what he thinks of the student body.
11. Ask a member of a fraternity/sorority on social probation what he/she thinks of the Dean of Men/Women or the Dean of Student Affairs. Then ask the dean what he/she thinks of the fraternity/sorority system.
12. Take the town's Chief of Police to lunch. Ask him anything.
13. After the admissions office shows you the best side of the campus, go to the campus coffee shop and ask the shaggiest beard to route you to the other side: the oldest dorm, the shabbiest classroom or lab, etc.

THEN . . . Remind yourself that you are in college to *learn,* in spite of all the human and material frailties you will put up with. Ignore (or meet with a sense of humor) the occasional disappointments and frustrations, but be alert to signs more subtle than the above—or to instances of poor-quality instruction.

REMEMBER . . . Basically, all education is *self*-education. It requires you and enough good books. The student who really wants to learn can get an education at *any* college that doesn't lock the library as you walk up the steps!

What It All Comes Down To

All of the months—even years—of preparation (the analysis of self, the college fairs attended, the campuses visited, and the interviews taken) come together with the completion of the application. It is *very* important for students to be certain that *all* of their submitted materials are prepared as thoroughly, thoughtfully, and creatively as possible. For some seniors, completing a set of applications is akin to having an additional course in their schedule.

Perhaps we should become more involved in advising students on application completion, thereby enabling our counselees to do a better job in completing these two- to six-page documents. But, admittedly, advising isn't always that easy. At times students will write directly to a college for an application, complete it, and then return it to the college without you seeing it, much less discussing it.

Much of the college application is cut-and-dried factual information, but our involvement with students could center on such issues as: the amount of time spent on application completion, the appropriate handling of optional questions, and the completeness of responses. The following items should prove beneficial as you work with your students on these topics.

■　　■　　■

Request for Autobiographical Sketch

_____

(Student Name)

Dear Counselee:

The responsibility of your counselor in preparing a "Secondary School Report" for colleges and universities is to provide a summary of your academic and extracurricular achievements. The counselor also presents some sense of your promise for further personal and intellectual growth. Conveying your unique qualities is not an easy task. Therefore, we would appreciate your giving us an honest estimation of yourself: what you have done and what you have left to do.

Please take the time to think about who you are and where you're headed. Don't limit your discussion to only what has happened to you in school. Include experiences drawn from any part of your life.

Thank you,

The Counseling Department

Personal Information Sheet

NAME: _____

1. What are your academic interests?

2. Which courses have you enjoyed the most?

3. Which courses have given you the most difficulty?

4. Which specific courses would you like to study in college?

5. What do you choose to learn when you can learn on your own? What do your choices show about your interests and the way you like to learn?

6. List the books you have read on your own in the past twelve months.

7. Describe an instance in which an article, book, play, or film has caused you to change your way of thinking.

8. What has been your most stimulating intellectual experience in recent years?

9. Is your high school academic record an accurate measure of your ability and potential? If not, what do you consider the best measure of your potential for success in college work?

10. What circumstances, if any, have interfered with your academic performance?

11. Has any summer experience, work, or study been of significant importance to you? Please describe.

12. Have you traveled or lived in different localities? Where? Comment on any significant travel experience(s).

13. What do you consider your greatest strengths?

14. What do you consider your greatest weaknesses?

15. Is there any other information you would like to share with your counselor in order that he/she can make an accurate appraisal of you to colleges and universities?

Parent "Brag Sheet"

PARENT "BRAG SHEET" FOR
COLLEGE RECOMMENDATION

Name of Student: _____

1. What do you consider to be your child's outstanding accomplishments during the past three or four years? Why did you select these as most important?

2. In what areas has your child shown the most development and growth during the past three or four years?

3. What do you consider to be his/her outstanding personality traits?

4. If you had to describe your son/daughter in five adjectives, what would they be?

5. Are there any unusual or personal circumstances that have affected your child's educational or personal experiences?

Please feel free to use a second sheet of paper if your comments do not fit into the space provided.

_____   _____
Name of Counselor   Parent Signature

Student "Brag Sheet"

STUDENT "BRAG SHEET" FOR
COLLEGE RECOMMENDATION

STUDENT NAME: _____

We believe that you should have a certain amount of input into the letters of recommendation that we write to colleges and universities on your behalf. Consequently, we are asking for your perceptions of your educational and personal growth.

Please respond to the following questions.

1. Are there any factors related to your grades that you would like colleges to be aware of?

2. Are there any factors about admission test scores that you would like us to address?

3. Are there any circumstances in your life that might have had a negative impact on your academic performance?

4. What are your proudest accomplishments?
   A. Academic?

   B. Personal?

5. List five adjectives that describe something about you as a person.

6. What extracurricular activity has been the most meaningful to you? Why?

7. What job experience has been especially meaningful? Why?

NOTE: Please feel free to use a second sheet of paper if your comments do not fit into the spaces provided.

_____   _____
Name of Counselor   Student Signature

Tips on Completing Activity and Employment Summary

TIPS ON COMPLETING ACTIVITY AND EMPLOYMENT SUMMARY

NOTE: Your completion of this form is voluntary, but we urge you to participate in this endeavor. Provide us with a completed master copy, from which we will make photocopies. The summary form will be forwarded *as submitted,* so make certain that the form represents you as you want to be represented. We will make certain that a photocopy accompanies each transcript you order for your selected colleges and universities.

1. Type the form, or have it typed.
2. Don't crowd the form! Double-space between activities.
3. Keep your entries to a reasonable number. Select your major activities and make them stand out; depth and consistency of involvement are the key factors here. (Some colleges and universities do not look for well-rounded students as much as they look to build well-rounded campuses.)
4. Include offices held, leadership displayed, and awards won. Set them out on separate lines so that they can be easily identified.
5. Don't underestimate your contributions. The seemingly unusual is often significant.
6. Remember that community involvement and employment are important factors.
7. Double-check your spelling.
8. Watch your abbreviations; their meanings may not always be evident.
9. Use a second sheet *if* necessary.

Activities and Employment Summary

ACTIVITIES AND EMPLOYMENT SUMMARY

Graduation Year: _____

Name: _____
          (Last)   (First)   (M.I.)

Address: _____
          (Street)   (Town)   (State, Zip)

SCHOOL/COMMUNITY ACTIVITIES AND AWARDS

(X denotes participation)

	9	10	11	12

Grade Level: 9 10 11 12

EMPLOYMENT RECORD

Employer Name	Job Position	Employed: From	To

Essay Tips

WHEN YOU WRITE YOUR ESSAY . . .

DO start early. Leave plenty of time to revise, reword, and rewrite. You *can* improve on your presentation.

DO read the directions carefully. You will want to answer the question as directly as possible, and you'll want to follow word limits exactly. Express yourself as briefly and as clearly as you can.

DO tell the truth about yourself. The admission committee is anonymous to you; you are completely unknown to it. Even if you run into a committee member in the future, he will have no way of connecting your essay (out of the thousands he has read) to you.

DO focus on an aspect of yourself that will show your best side. You might have overcome some adversity, worked through a difficult project, or profited from a specific incident. A narrow focus is more interesting than broad-based generalizations.

DO feel comfortable in expressing anxieties. Everybody has them, and it's good to know that an applicant can see them and face them.

DO tie yourself to the college. Be specific about what this particular school can do for you. Your essay can have different slants for different colleges.

DO speak positively. Negatives tend to turn people off.

DO write about your greatest assets and achievements. You *should* be proud of them!

But . . .

DON'T repeat information given elsewhere on your application. The committee has already seen it—and it looks as though you have nothing better to say.

DON'T write on general, impersonal topics—like the nuclear arms race or the importance of good management in business. The college wants to know about *you.*

DON'T use the personal statement to excuse your shortcomings. It would give them additional attention.

DON'T use cliches.

(Essay Tips, continued)

DON'T go to extremes: too witty, too opinionated, or too "intellectual."

Remember:

The personal statement is YOURS. If it looks like Madison Avenue, the admission committee will probably assume that it is your mother's or your father's or their secretaries' work.

A "gimmick" essay rarely goes anywhere. The committee may be amused but unimpressed with your candidacy.

Write a serious essay, from the bottom of your heart, in the most mature manner possible.

Teacher Recommendation Form

TEACHER RECOMMENDATION FORM

To Be Completed by Student:

STUDENT NAME _____ GRADUATION YEAR _____

PROSPECTIVE COLLEGE _____

ADDRESS _____

To Be Completed by Person Making Recommendation:

EVALUATOR _____ TITLE _____

COURSE/ACTIVITY _____ YEAR _____

Please give your candid estimate of the above student's academic performance, intellectual promise, and personal qualities. Please provide specific examples where possible.

Composite Recommendation Request

A composite recommendation is an approach you can take in those cases in which you are not too knowledgeable about your counselee. You work the recommendation up after you have received impressions from two or three staff members who are involved with the student (teachers, coaches, advisors).

■　　　■　　　■

COMPOSITE RECOMMENDATION REQUEST

DATE: _____

TO:　　Teacher

FROM: Jack Stafford, Counselor

RE:　　College Recommendation

_____ is working on her applications for
　　　　　(Student name)
college and gave your name as a resource person for my recommendation. Any open-ended comments (of about fifty words) that you feel are appropriate would be most helpful to me in completing my task.

Thank You!

Selecting Teachers to Recommend You

GUIDANCE DEPARTMENT
HIGHLAND PARK HIGH SCHOOL
HIGHLAND PARK, ILLINOIS 60035

RECOMMENDATIONS: CHOOSING TEACHERS WHO WILL HELP YOU

Directions:

1. Make a list of all the adjectives you would like teachers to use to describe you.

2. Set up a piece of paper with five or six columns.

List adjectives here:	Teacher:	Teacher:	Teacher:	Teacher:

3. Arrange the adjectives in *descending order of priority* in the first column.

4. List potential teachers in the other columns across the page. Place a check in the proper box for every adjective a particular teacher could use to describe you.

5. Select the two or three teachers with the greatest number of checks, provided that the checks are for items you really want covered in the recommendation.

6. Arrange a separate piece of paper for each of these teachers. On the left of the page, list the adjectives that you want the teacher to use; then give an example of your performance that illustrates that adjective.

7. Approach the teacher and explain your request. If the teacher agrees to recommend you, settle on a timetable and give the teacher a preaddressed, stamped envelope.

8. If you are making the request for several schools, tell the teacher *at that time* so that copies of the recommendation can be made.

Helping Families with Financial Aid

We continue to try to identify and educate more of the nation's talented, but we do so with considerably less financial support from the federal government. Consequently, everyone else has been asked to shoulder more financial responsibility for the post-secondary education of our youth—especially parents.

College costs are skyrocketing, and they are outpacing inflation 2 to 1. The potential couldn't be greater for school counselors to render support to families in their quest to make that "best match" a reality. Simply doing an effective job of counseling on the basics of financial aid has taken on added importance for counselors. For example, today it is critical that families distinguish between the *price* of an institution and the actual *cost*. Often, if the initial price looks too great, families won't explore further. Parents need to know that many private colleges and universities in this country have some very innovative financial aid programs in place.

Of course, to qualify for financial assistance a family must show financial necessity: A family does not have to be poor to qualify for aid, but it must demonstrate a real need for it.

■   ■   ■

Worksheet for Analyzing College Expenses

WORKSHEET FOR ANALYZING COLLEGE EXPENSES

Expenses	*College A*	*College B*	*College C*
Tuition			
Room			
Board			
Required Fees			
Voluntary Fees			
Supplies			
Textbooks			
Insurance			
Transportation			
Personal Expenses			

Questions to Raise with a Financial Aid Matching Service

Monies for higher education have become so tight that families are turning to financial aid "matchmakers" in greater numbers than ever before. The number of these computerized matching-service firms has increased significantly as well. Since the first company opened its door some twenty-five years ago, the advertising message has remained the same: "Big dollars are going begging. There are literally millions of unclaimed dollars just waiting for you and others like you."

But you might want to counsel your families: Buyer beware! A study of over fifty firms by the California Student Aid Commission that utilized a test group of high school students revealed that not one firm provided effective matching. Researchers say that the claim that significant amounts of educational monies are going untapped is unproved. If a family does not have the time to conduct a meaningful search of its own, however, before contracting with a particular firm they might want to obtain answers to a few questions.

■   ■   ■

QUESTIONS TO RAISE WITH A FINANCIAL
AID MATCHING SERVICE

1. What is the size of the financial aid source data bank?

2. How many leads will the company supply for the fee? How many of these leads are in the form of scholarships, grants, loans, work-study programs, or contests?

3. In supplying its leads, will the company be duplicating state and national programs for which students will already be considered through normal financial aid channels?

4. Does the company periodically update its files as to eligibility requirements, application deadlines, etc.?

5. What has been the track record of the company? In other words, how successful have former participants been in securing financial aid from company-recommended sources?

6. What is the company's refund policy? Will it return all or a portion of the paid fee if the client is not satisfied with its services?

Invitation to Financial Aid Workshop

EAST BRUNSWICK HIGH SCHOOL
380 CRANBURY ROAD
EAST BRUNSWICK, NJ 08816

January 19, 19———

Dear Parents:

The Counseling Department has arranged a special meeting to help parents with the New Jersey Financial Aid Form. William Daley, president of the College Financial Aid Company, Sparta, New Jersey, will discuss the completion of the required forms. He will also offer some alternative routes for financial aid.

The session will be held February 1, 19——— in the high school cafeteria and will begin promptly at 7:30 P.M. Bring your figures so that you can work along with Mr. Daley. (NJFAF forms will be available.)

The meeting last year was most helpful to the people who attended; this year's session should be equally informative. We look forward to seeing you at this important event.

Sincerely,

Curtis Lippincott
College Counselor

"How to Survive in College" Workshop Plan

HAMILTON TOWNSHIP SCHOOL DISTRICT
HAMILTON HIGH SCHOOL NORTH—NOTTINGHAM
TRENTON, NEW JERSEY 08619

"How to Survive in College" Workshop

I. Objectives
  A. Participants will develop an awareness of the various issues that must be dealt with as a college freshman.
  B. Participants will recognize their values before having to act on them.
  C. Participants will become aware of the need for time management and planning as a college freshman.

II. Procedures
  A. Conduct workshop in all A-level American Government and Economics classes.
  B. Visit B-level sections for sign-up.
    1. Clear date with teacher.
    2. Procure empty classroom for B-level groups.
  C. Conduct workshop based on Elon College, NC, video, "How to Survive in College."
  D. About one week after workshop, conduct a get-together with seniors and several returning college freshmen, who can speak about their collegiate experiences.

Invitation to Returning Graduates

As a follow-up program to the "How to Survive in College" workshop, each year the Nottingham counselors invite a half dozen or so returning graduates to participate on an informal panel.

■   ■   ■

HAMILTON TOWNSHIP SCHOOL DISTRICT
HAMILTON HIGH SCHOOL NORTH—NOTTINGHAM
TRENTON, NEW JERSEY 08619

Date: _____

Dear _____,

Congratulations! You survived your first year of college. How about coming back to Nottingham to share your first-year experiences with our current seniors?

On Thursday, May 28, from 1:30 to 2:30 the Counseling Department is hosting a get-together. We would like to see you and to hear the inside scoop on what it's really like to be a college freshman.

Enclosed is a list of adjustment issues about which our seniors may well be concerned. You might want to take a moment to reflect on these issues before your arrival on May 28. Candor is the key word.

If you can join us, please telephone Mrs. Schweder or Mrs. White at 587-1873 by Friday, May 22.

We look forward to hearing from you.

Sincerely,

Nottingham Counselors

College Adjustment Issues for Discussion

COLLEGE ADJUSTMENT ISSUES

_____ First week of college

_____ Roommate

_____ Social life

_____ Friends

_____ Peer pressure

_____ Dormitory life

_____ Noise

_____ Best time/place to study

_____ Time management

_____ Food (quality and quantity)

_____ Homesickness

_____ Course selection and load

_____ Professors

_____ College work vs. high school work

_____ Responsibilities

_____ Other adjustment problems

_____ Biggest adjustment problem

What is the one thing you wish you had known *before* you went away to college?

Alumni Follow-Up Survey

ALUMNI FOLLOW-UP SURVEY

I. Which college or university are you currently attending?

_____

II. How would you rate its academic program?

	Excellent	Adequate	Insufficient
Interesting?	_____	_____	_____
Diversified?	_____	_____	_____
Challenging?	_____	_____	_____
Faculty accessibility?	_____	_____	_____
Facilities?	_____	_____	_____
Advising?	_____	_____	_____
Class size?	_____	_____	_____

III. How would you rate the nonacademic aspects of the college?

	Excellent	Adequate	Insufficient
Clubs/Extracurricular?	_____	_____	_____
Athletics?	_____	_____	_____
Recreation?	_____	_____	_____
Social life?	_____	_____	_____
Friendliness?	_____	_____	_____
Housing?	_____	_____	_____
School spirit?	_____	_____	_____

IV. What do you like most about your college?

V. What do you like least?

Alumni College Evaluation Report

WATCHUNG HILLS REGIONAL HIGH SCHOOL
WARREN, NEW JERSEY

ALUMNI COLLEGE EVALUATION REPORT

You have experienced education both at WHRHS and at your present college, so you are in a unique position to advise future graduates about your college. Your fair and candid answers to these questions will be made available to the students of WHRHS.

NAME: _____ WHRHS class of: _____ College: _____

Major (if known): _____

In what ways (if at all) is the college most *different* from what you had expected?

What do you wish you had known about this college *before* you arrived?

What do you like best about your college?

How is the college expected to change in the next few years?

How would you describe the atmosphere on campus?

Which departments appear to be the strongest and most popular?

Which departments seem to be relatively small, unpopular, or academically limited?

What are the "burning issues" on campus now (i.e., concerns voiced by student government or newspaper)?

How would you characterize student morale? Faculty morale?

What type of person would *not* be happy there?

What type of person *would* be quite happy there?

What values seem to be most important to the majority of the students?

What does the campus *lack* most at present?

What is the most *distinctive* thing about your college?

(Alumni College Evaluation Report, continued)

Where would you place your *ability,* compared to the average student there?

How would you compare your high school preparation to the average there?

How could WHRHS better prepare students for this college?

In a word or two, describe your college in terms of:

Social life

Athletic program

Academic standards

Cultural opportunities

Rules and regulations

School spirit

Freshman life and program

Quality of instruction

Consultant to Counselor Memo

The many advantages of close communication between specialist and generalist should be obvious.

■   ■   ■

Date: _____

To: Ken Franklin, Counselor

From: Ed Goldstein, College Consultant

I just want to let you know that I plan to meet with your counselee, _____, and her parents in the near future.

If you have any input, please contact me. I'll share the results of our discussion with you.

Faculty Workshop: Writing College Recommendations

FACULTY WORKSHOP: WRITING COLLEGE RECOMMENDATIONS

I. Are Recommendations Important, and Do Admissions People Really Read Them?

II. Getting Prepared to Recommend
   A. Negotiating with the student
   B. Engaging in a bit of research
   C. Considering possible constraints
   D. Deciding on voice and tone

III. The Anatomy of a "Solid" Recommendation
   A. Credibility
   B. Specificity
   C. Academic Considerations
      1. Conceptual ability
      2. Organizational ability
      3. Extent of oral and written expression
      4. Ability to read with perceptivity
      5. Additional talents and skills
      6. Overall quality of academic program
   D. Personal Qualities
      1. Honesty
      2. Emotional and social maturity
      3. Leadership capability
      4. Capacity for growth
      5. Ability to take and profit from criticism
   E. Extracurricular Participation
      1. Role of the teacher, if any
      2. "Litanizing" versus enhancing
   F. Setting up the Anecdote(s)

IV. Things to Avoid
   A. "Seat of the Pants" Writing
   B. Inappropriate Medical Statements
   C. Emotional Comments
   D. Negative Remarks of Past Decisions Made by Collegiate Institution

(Faculty Workshop: Writing College Recommendations, continued)

    E. Negative Remarks About the Form or the Admissions Process in General

    F. Flowery Prose That Draws Attention to Itself

Suggested Reading

Hayden, Thomas. *Writing Effective College Recommendations: A Guide for Teachers.* Princeton, NJ: Peterson's Guides, Inc., 1983. (a pamphlet)

College Admissions Guides Order Form

DATE: June 1, 19_____

TO: All Counselors

FROM: Martha Livingston, Chairperson

RE: College Admission Guides

Please list the titles of four (4) comprehensive or specialty guides related to the college admission process that you would like ordered for your personal use for the coming academic year.

I would appreciate receiving your list by Thursday, June 7.

Counselor: _____

IV. Communication and Professional Development ____

Communication is the tie that binds. Within a school counseling program, communication can bind a group of people—student, parents, teachers, counselor—into a unit working for the positive developmental growth of the youngster.

Communication can occur in several ways. Conferences can be arranged so that several people can participate in the solution of a problem. Parents can be notified about a broad range of issues, from the academic progress of their child to the availability of schoolwide programs. The community can be contacted as well. And it is critical to communicate fully and freely with teachers, for the good of each student and for the good of the school.

Another form of communication is vital in your professional role as counselor: You must be open to ideas, techniques, and insights from other counselors. Like everyone else in the educational system, your professional approach must be evaluated so that it can improve.

The ideas presented in this section should assist you in your quest to improve professionally.

13. CONFERENCES

The words "confer" and "counselor" are essentially synonymous—school counselors are forever conferring with someone or another.

Face-to-face parent/counselor conferences can be an especially valuable tool for greater parental understanding of student behavior and achievement. The ideal setting, of course, is with both parents present. Having two parents in attendance has obvious advantages, including the chance for you to observe family dynamics. Some professionals believe that certain crucial problems mandate the presence of both parents.

Dealing with today's "mixed" families (custodial parent, shared custody, remarried parent(s), single parent, etc.) requires a great deal of thought and care. It may be beneficial to contact the parent without custody, too, or the custodial parent *and* the stepparent.

Periodic get-togethers with parents serve three purposes:

1. Parents learn about the student's activities and scholastic progress. The more information we place in parents' hands, the better.
2. Parents more fully appreciate the efforts that the school is making to help the youngsters achieve.

3. Contact with the home is an opportunity for counselors to acquire parental cooperation and support.

There will be times when you will want to meet, wholly or in part, with a parent without the student present. The decision to include or exclude a student is an important one and should be well-thought out in advance of any meeting. Having your counselee present has the advantage of the student's response to questions or contribution to the development of a cooperative plan of action.

Setting up a case conference is a real challenge: It would be a real rarity to find student, parents, and all affected teachers free at the same time. Still, no matter what the time of day, a case conference can be an extremely beneficial communications vehicle.

The material in this topic covers parent, teacher, and case conferences.

Case Conference Anecdotal Record

However brief a case conference may be, parents welcome the opportunity to meet with all of their youngster's teachers at once. Both teachers and parents get to share concerns and findings; counselors get to hear more about the counselee's involvement in the classroom. Many counselors spend additional postconference time meeting privately with parents in order to summarize and advise.

Here is an anecdotal report sheet that can also be adapted to a file card format. Information gathered can be useful in one-to-one or case conferences.

■　　　■　　　■

HAMILTON MIDDLE SCHOOL

COUNSELOR'S CORNER　　　　　　　　　*ANECDOTAL RECORD*

STUDENT: ——————————————— DATE: —————————

UNIT: ——————————— GRADE: —————

PROBLEM: ————————————————————————————

————————————————————————————————

AFFECTED STAFF MEMBERS/PEERS: —————————————————

SUMMARY:

COUNSELOR: ———————————————

Case Conference Notes

CASE CONFERENCE NOTES

Student: _____   Date: _____

Student ID#: _____

Members in Attendance: _____

_____

_____

SUMMARY OF DISCUSSION:

RECOMMENDATIONS:

FOLLOW-UP:

_____
Counselor

Conference Comments Card

This all-purpose form may be used to record brief notes about a given student. The form can be placed in the student's folder or attached to a file card.

■   ■   ■

CONFERENCE COMMENTS

Student Name: _____

Dates   Comments

_____

_____

_____

_____

_____

_____

Teacher Notice of Conference

Some counselors have great track records in getting all invited teachers to their case conferences. Meetings are kept moving—they usually last no more than fifteen minutes—while discussion is kept to the point. Furthermore, if a teacher cannot attend, he or she is asked to submit a written report. These counselors have found that teachers, who value their free or planning time more than ever these days, are happier to cooperate with this kind of professional approach.

Note the tone of the following memorandum: the "we're in it together" attitude exemplified by the use of the words "meet with us"; the diplomatic approach taken through employment of the term "appreciate"; and the "keeping things tight" posture by the request for notification of nonattendance.

■　　■　　■

SOMERVILLE JUNIOR HIGH SCHOOL
COUNSELING DEPARTMENT

DATE: _____

TO:　　Mr. Walters
　　　　Ms. Dickinson
　　　　Mr. Shook
　　　　Mr. Elgin
　　　　Ms. DeAngelo

FROM: Robert Senick, Counselor

RE: _____

Mr. and Mrs. _____ would like to meet with us on Wednesday, October 11, at 2:15, here in the Counseling Office to discuss _____'s academic work to date. If, for some reason, you cannot be present, I would appreciate it if you would notify me in advance and at the same time provide me with a brief written evaluation of _____'s progress this first quarter.

Thank You!

Teacher Notice of Conference, variation

NOTICE OF CONFERENCE

TO: _____   DATE: _____
                (Teacher)

RE: _____
                (Student)

A conference concerning this student's academic progress has been scheduled in the

Counseling Office on _____ at _____.
                            (Date)   (Time)

A parent (will) (will not) be present.

Your presence would be greatly appreciated!

Thanks.

                              _____
                                        Counselor

Request to Parent for Conference

THAYER ELEMENTARY SCHOOL
MAIN STREET
MONMOUTH, OR 97361

Date: _____

Dear Parent,

It is most important that I meet with you on one of the two conference days established for Thayer Elementary School, February 27 or 28, in regard to your child's progress. This conference is necessary because:

_____

_____

Please call the Counseling Office for an appointment at 650-6770.

Sincerely yours,

_____

Ruth Mitchell
Counselor

Request from Parent for Conference

PARENT REQUEST FOR CONFERENCE

Date: _____

Parent(s) Name: _____

Student Name: _____

Teacher Name: _____

Telephone Number: (home) _____

(office) _____

Reason(s) for Conference: _____

_____

_____

14. COMMUNICATING WITH TEACHERS

Let it suffice to say that the most important people you work with—after your students—are those most involved with the welfare of your students: the teachers.

One reason for developing sound communications with the teaching faculty is that they can be wonderful sources of information. Take any instructional department: The combined experiential knowledge of all the teachers is mind-boggling. You and your counselees would do well to tap into this rich, supplemental source for guidance in selecting the proper courses to take. Teachers can tell you the respective levels of difficulty, give a more detailed analysis of specific courses, and be an excellent resource when exploring particular college majors and occupational fields. You will have to weigh specific teacher recommendations carefully, though, since any particular subject will have to fit the program of the "whole" student.

Whether teachers are willing to fully communicate with counselors can depend on the amount of rapport established between counselor and teacher. Call it a "comfort" factor if you will. Counselors often reach out to various teachers, but are the teachers comfortable in going to counselors?

Some teachers *want* to gather background information on their students, especially those they suspect are not working up to their ability. Others seek an advocate to help them solve a student's problem. We see "comfortable" teachers making frequent visits to the Counseling Office. It could be that these frequent visitors are more at ease with counseling services than some of their colleagues, and they are often easier to deal with on a daily basis. This can be the rationale for developing both rapport-building programs and quality orientation programs.

There are little techniques that help, like follow-up notes. When a teacher comes to you with a student problem and you've told her that you'll take some specific action, *be sure to do so promptly*. Then, write a brief memo to the teacher thanking her for her interest and informing her that you have indeed taken action.

Like anyone else, a teacher needs some stroking. Counselors who relate well to classroom teachers are often the ones who in some way or another convey a strong message of "I respect you, and I admire the quality of your teaching."

Remember: A teacher with positive feelings about counselors can share these same feelings with hundreds of different students.

Teacher-Counselor Communication Form

TEACHER-COUNSELOR COMMUNIQUÉ

DATE: _____

TO: _____   COULD WE PLEASE HAVE YOUR

FROM: _____   REPLY BY _____?

RE: _____

_____ Please telephone the parent at your earliest convenience

Phone #:

Best times:

Concerning:

_____ Please contact me at your convenience about this student. Thanks.

_____ Please plan to attend a brief but important meeting about this student on

_____ at _____ o'clock in _____.

_____ Please use the back of this page to suggest homework assignments for this

student, who will be absent from school for the next _____ days.

_____ Please share with us your current evaluation of this student's progress in the
areas circled below. Note that the parent(s) will see your remarks.

ACHIEVEMENT:

EFFORT AND HOMEWORK:

ATTITUDE AND EMOTIONS:

RELIABILITY/SOCIABILITY/MORALE:

CHANGES (IF ANY) DURING THE PAST _____ WEEK(S):

Thank you very much for your help!

Notice to Teachers of Student's Loss

_____
Date

Dear Colleague:

I have been informed that _____ has just experienced a death in the family: _____ has recently passed on.

As you know, death can be a shattering event. The age of the youngster, the emotional ties with the deceased, and the circumstances surrounding the death all affect the depth and duration of grief. It will take some time for _____ to get back to "normal."

Your sympathetic welcome and special understanding will be a tremendous help to your student during the period of adjustment that must follow.

Please let me know how he/she is doing. We can work together to help the youngster during this difficult period.

Thanks!

_____
Counselor

Passing on a Compliment

Sometimes current or former counselees make positive remarks about a particular teacher to a counselor. It's nice to pass on the compliment!

■   ■   ■

_____
(Date)

Dear _____:
     (Name of Teacher)

I just wanted you to know that _____ told me what a great job you did with Calculus I in preparing him for his first college math course. He really appreciates it.

Sincerely,

_____
Walter Denman
Counselor

Thank-You Letter from Counseling Department

DEMARCK SENIOR HIGH SCHOOL
2000 WETHERBY PLACE
DETROIT, MICHIGAN

June 10, 1990

Dear Colleague:

The Counseling Department would like to express its thanks to you for all the help you have given the students during the current school year. No one department has an exclusive on the word "counsel"; the whole faculty is involved. And as part of that team, your effort has been extraordinary; you have often gone far beyond the line of duty.

We especially want to commend you for your participation in the college admission process. You have advised students on particular schools and majors; you have counseled them as teacher, coach, advisor, and friend. You also have advised us as to a student's special needs and difficulties, and you have even given your present and former students written recommendations to help them get accepted to the colleges of their choice.

You know how hard you have worked. We know, too.

Sincerely,

The Counselors

Thank-You for Participation in Testing Program

Sometimes one or two counselors are placed in charge of an all-school testing program. It is appropriate for the individuals involved to send a thank-you note to the faculty; in fact, it can be a nice personal touch.

■   ■   ■

Dear Fellow Faculty Members:

Peg Hamilton and I would like to thank you for your participation in this spring's CTBS testing program.

The organization and supervision of such a large-scale program carries with it a certain amount of anxiety. Your pleasant manner and helpful attitude went a long way toward allaying our fears; whenever a problem surfaced and we asked for your assistance, your reaction was both positive and instantaneous. As a result, we all produced a successful program.

Again, thank you for your efforts!

Sincerely,

_____

Robert Stenson and Peg Hamilton
Counselors

Referral Feedback Form

Staff often feel "left out in the cold" once they have made a referral to a student assistance program or another in-school committee. Appraising them of the initial action taken on a particular referral increases their continued cooperation and support.

■   ■   ■

REFERRAL FEEDBACK FORM

Date: _____

To: _____

From: _____

Re: Status of Your Referral of _____
(student name)

Thank you for your recent referral. The item(s) checked below indicates the current status of this individual.

[ ]   Student has been referred to a support group within the school.

[ ]   Student has been referred to a peer listener.

[ ]   Home has been contacted.

[ ]   In-school assessment process has begun. Input from other staff has been requested.

[ ]   Student has been referred to a community agency for assessment and/or evaluation.

[ ]   Student is now involved in periodic counseling sessions with his/her counselor.

[ ]   Student has been referred to a treatment/rehabilitation program and will be absent from classes until further notice.

[ ]   Our assessment indicates that no further action is needed at this time.

[ ]   Other: _____
_____

Counselor Liaison to Department

A novel and worthwhile idea is to assign counselors as liaisons to subject-area departments. Improved interdepartmental communications and relationships can be derived from such an arrangement. Giving each counselor the choice of subject-area departments may be the way to start the program. This concept works especially well where a counseling department is staffed with enough counselors to cover all the subject-area departments.

■   ■   ■

_____
                                                    (Date)

Dear _____:
                (Department Chairperson)

We have just established a special program whereby a designated counselor will serve as a liaison between the Counseling Department and a particular subject-area department.

The purpose of this arrangement is to improve communications and relationships between Counseling and the various subject areas. I will be the liaison to your department for the current school year.

Would it be possible for me to attend one or two of your department meetings for the purpose of exchanging information and discussing matters of mutual concern?

I look forward to hearing from you.

Sincerely,

_____
                                            Counselor

Teacher-Initiated Drop Request

Dropping a class should not always be a one-way street. There are those rare moments when a teacher has "had it." If it's not too late in the term, the student can pick up another course; otherwise he/she can go to a study hall.

■   ■   ■

TEACHER-INITIATED DROP REQUEST

_____
Date

To Whom It May Concern:

I would like to recommend that _____
Name of Student

be dropped from my course, _____.
Course Title

A meeting with the affected student and his or her parent/guardian has been conducted concerning this proposal. The reasons for my recommending the drop are as follows:

_____

_____

_____
Teacher Signature

I have reviewed this proposal and recommend the following:

_____

_____

_____
Supervisor Signature

I have conferred with the student, parent/guardian, and teacher and recommend the following: _____

_____

_____

_____
Counselor Signature

15. COMMUNICATING WITH PARENTS AND THE COMMUNITY

Developmental issues, such as searching for one's own identity or seeking to become more independent, are often heightened by parents' lack of understanding of the many changes their children are undergoing. Mom and Dad don't always know how to adjust their parenting styles to match a given situation and, consequently, they experience serious problems with their children. In such cases, parents could no doubt profit from your professional help. Many parents face the greatest challenges of their parenting careers at a time when their skills are most dated and least appropriate.

You can develop programs that can be presented to parents as a means of preparing them to cope with such problems as family difficulties, separations, sexuality, and substance abuse before any of these problems becomes an issue for their children.

Counselors can help parents to effectively encourage and promote proper growth by consulting with them individually or in groups.

There are several options available to you when working with groups:

- Use a prepackaged program. Warning: Any prepackaged program should be screened to make sure it meets the special needs of a community.
- Conduct a discussion group with a loosely organized format. On the one hand, this type of program would be responsive to the specific needs of the participants; on the other hand, there is the danger of too much time being devoted to some issues to the exclusion of others. There is also the likelihood of under-stressing the skill-building techniques.
- Develop your own program. This option has the advantage of applicability to community needs, and the disadvantage of time consumption in preparation.

No matter what option you choose, it is imperative that any program (1) underscores the significance of solid communication between parents and youngster; (2) emphasizes the need for mutual respect on the part of both parties; and (3) stresses the importance of allowing young people to assume an increasing amount of responsibility for their own behavior as they mature.

It is with parents that a counselor's human relations skills need be the sharpest. Many letters and notices to parents have been included in other topics to hone those skills. In this topic, you will find an additional assortment of home/school communication pieces as well as some worthwhile field-tested programs.

Invitation to Summer Orientation

Date: _____

Dear Parents:

You, as the parents of an incoming freshman student, are cordially invited to visit the high school this summer. During this visit, I will conduct a program designed to orient both you and your youngster to high school services that are available, with special emphasis on counseling programs. A portion of the presentation will be spent taking a tour of building facilities and grounds.

It is most important that your son/daughter attend this session with you. You will be meeting in a small group with other parents and students. The session will last approximately one hour.

I look forward to meeting you at the time and date listed below.

Sincerely,

_____

Walter Harrison
Counselor

MEETING TIME: 9:00 A.M.

DATE: August 4

ROOM: Library

Letter of Introduction

MIDDLESEX HIGH SCHOOL
MIDDLESEX, NEW JERSEY 08846

Date: _____

Dear Mr./Mrs. _____:

I would like to take this opportunity to introduce myself to you as
_____'s counselor for the next four years. I look forward to work-
ing closely with him/her, and I will make every effort to see to it that your
youngster receives as much personal assistance as possible. We want the
high school years to be rewarding and profitable.

The Counseling Department looks forward to continual communication
with parents; I invite you to contact me at any time. I can be reached at
968-0202.

I hope to meet with you some time in the near future.

Sincerely,

_____
Counselor

Letter Describing Counseling Services

This letter advertises counseling services to the parents of incoming ninth graders.

■   ■   ■

Dear Parents:

In an effort to more fully meet the needs of its students, Ocean View High School has a complete staff of certified counselors who stand ready to assist your son or daughter in dealing with a wide range of issues, including those of academics, career exploration, personal problems, and college admission.

A student may request to see his or her counselor *at any time;* or, as the parent, an occasion might arise when you would ask the counselor to send for your youngster. In any case, every student is seen at least twice during the academic year as a matter of policy.

If you have questions or concerns, don't hesitate to telephone us here at the Counseling Office.

We look forward to helping your son or daughter.

Sincerely,

Jonathan Davies
Director of Counseling

Letter: Getting Off to a Good Start

OFF AND RUNNING?

Dear Parent/Guardian:

It is important that you help your child get off to a good start this school year. Here are six ways that might help *you* get started.

1. Get to know your child's teacher as soon as possible. You know your child best. Share your knowledge with the teacher. Does your child have a special interest? Are there areas where you see your child needing special help? Don't wait until parent conference time to make that all-important contact.

2. Don't hesitate to speak with the teacher about sensitive issues. Remember that what goes on at home can affect the student's performance in the classroom. Indeed, parental separation, a new baby, family illness, or even a change of residence, can have a harmful effect on a student's schoolwork.

3. Please make certain that your child gets enough rest. Tired children cannot do their best work. Consistency is the key here: Set a bedtime hour, and stick to it.

4. Be familiar with what the school expects of your child, e.g., how much homework will there be?

5. Limit television watching. Study after study concludes that those children who do the best in school watch the least TV.

6. Please don't hesitate to telephone me here at the Counseling Office if you have any questions or concerns. I am here to help you resolve your problems.

Sincerely,

Lois R. Medina
Counselor

Tips for Parents

SUPPORT YOUR CHILD

Your child wants to succeed in school. With these ten tips in mind, you can increase your support of your very special youngster.

1. Periodically (but not continuously) communicate to your child the importance of education.

2. Build up your child's confidence and self-esteem.

3. Work with your child to help him or her develop a positive attitude toward work and school.

4. Provide encouragement to your child whenever possible.

5. Be a good listener.

6. Be available to discuss problems your child is having, whether they are large or small.

7. Set up your child's time schedule to include a balance of work, play, and study.

8. Establish a time for sharing and caring.

9. Take part in your child's education—be active in his or her school.

10. Show your love and affection to your child—often!

Homework/Study Guidelines for Parents

The homework process may well be the most important contact parents have with a school. It is critical, therefore, that a homework/study policy be continually reviewed and in place at the beginning of each academic year. Furthermore, the policy needs to be communicated effectively to *both* teachers and parents: *Everyone* needs to be on base as to a school's homework/study expectations.

Getting the word to parents can be accomplished at orientation meetings, as part of a message in the school bulletin, as an article in the PTA newsletter, or by way of an open letter from the Counseling Department.

■   ■   ■

Homework/Study Guidelines

Dear Parent/Guardian:

Homework serves an important function in your youngster's school life. It is a means for the student to review and reinforce the lessons taught in school. It is also a method by which a youngster can develop sound work and study habits that will assist him or her throughout the remaining school years.

As a parent, you are a vital link to the school in a homework/study program that includes helping your youngster develop routines to successfully handle assigned homework. We offer the following tips, as you work with your youngster.

1. Always ask your child if he/she has homework on a given day. Homework is generally assigned Monday through Thursday, except for holiday periods. (Older children often have long-term assignments that require work on holidays or weekends.) Asking him/her every day will help the youngster develop a habit of self-inquiry.

2. Be interested in the homework. Seeing what he/she is doing helps in two ways: You can get a sense of the child's progress in various subject areas; your youngster will sense that homework is important and that you care about his/her efforts.

3. Homework is the child's work, not yours. Be sure that he/she does it himself or herself. If the youngster has difficulty, write a note to the teacher; the teacher can then make the proper adjustments, such as making the assignment more clear, providing more practice in class, explaining in a different manner, etc.

4. Set up a time for homework that is acceptable for your particular family routine, and teach your child to fulfill that commitment.

5. Make sure your child has a quiet place to study and is unhampered by other people and their activities.

Learning to work well at homework increases your youngster's self-esteem: He/she has a responsibility that when fulfilled means success!

How Parents Can Build Self-Esteem

Ten Tips: How Parents Can Build Self-Esteem

1. *It's patience and tolerance that count!* "You seem discouraged. Let's go over your mistakes together so that you'll be able to avoid them next time."

2. *Emphasize what your youngster does right.* "Until now you've been doing just fine. Let's see if we can get you back on track."

3. *Support self-expression and creativity.* "You've prepared your report in an unusual manner, but you'll want to make certain that you have adequately supported your findings with the proper research."

4. *Success with new learning experiences often calls for a well-developed plan of attack.* "Let's break this project down into smaller, more manageable components so that it doesn't seem so overwhelming."

5. *Make time to communicate with your youngster.* "How did school go today? What did you learn?"

6. *Positive, constructive criticism is the way to go.* "Great! This report has many good ideas. You might want to arrange your thoughts a bit better, though."

7. *Compare your youngster's progress to his/her own record.* "Let's not worry about your friend's test grade. It's *you* and your achievement that I care about."

8. *Avoid labeling!* Off-handed comments can seriously damage self-esteem. DON'T say: "Jim never takes time to read directions."

9. *Focus on the here and now.* "I'm happy to see that you'll be turning your report in on time."

10. *Continue to expect an increase in accomplishment.* "It looks like a tough assignment, but with all that you have accomplished so far, I know you can do it."

Invitation to "Coffee and Conversation"

Date: _____

Dear Parent/Guardian:

In celebration of National School Counseling Week, you are cordially invited for "Coffee and Conversation" with the counselors.

Date: Wednesday, February 8

Time: 2:30–3:30 P.M.

Location: Faculty Room

Please plan to stop by for an informal chat. We would enjoy meeting you here at the Weber School.

Notice of Parent/Teacher Conferences

Today it's more than just back-to-school nights. A program that was once reserved for elementary school students has now become standard procedure: a series of parent/teacher conferences at the secondary level as well. Note the advertising of school counselor availability.

■   ■   ■

Date: _____

Dear Parent/Guardian:

Millbrook High School will conduct Parent/Teacher Conferences on November 26, 27, and 28. To accommodate all parents, as well as to prevent delays in visiting with your youngster's teachers, it is necessary for you to reserve conference time. Individual conferences will be limited to fifteen minutes.

On Tuesday, November 26, conferences will be held from 5:00 P.M. to 9:00 P.M. On Wednesday, November 27 and Thursday, November 28, conferences will be held from 12:30 P.M. until 3:00 P.M.

Please telephone the high school to arrange as many appointment periods as necessary. Prior to telephoning, please refer to the enclosed map and teacher-assigned room chart to assist you in establishing the order in which you would like to see the teachers.

It will also be possible for you to make an appointment to speak with your youngster's counselor. These appointments should be made directly through the Counseling Office.

We look forward to seeing you.

Sincerely,

_____
Ross D. Buffalino
Assistant Principal

Program for Parents of Freshmen

Port Clinton High School, Port Clinton, Ohio, invites the parents of ninth graders to an unusual informational program about four weeks after the commencement of the school year. The format of "How Is Your Freshman Doing?" includes sophomore students who describe what it was like being a freshman; teachers who discuss course work, study habits, and the importance of solid teacher-parent communication; and a question-and-answer period moderated by members of the Counseling Department.

■   ■   ■

Port Clinton High School Guidance Department
presents
"HOW IS YOUR FRESHMAN DOING?"
One of a series of informational programs for students,
parents, and the public of the Port Clinton City Schools
Wednesday, September 28, 19____

PROGRAM

Welcome:	George Scheckelhoff Assistant Principal
Opening Remarks:	Thomas Brown Guidance Director
Sophomore Student Speakers:	Brad Kocher Heather Mann
Ninth-Grade Teachers:	Ms. Schweitzer English
	Ms. Wilson Foreign Language
	Ms. Telloni Mathematics
	Mrs. Rusincovitch Science
	Mr. Link Science
	Mr. Radloff General Business

Question-and-Answer Period
Refreshments

Invitation to Program for Parents of Freshmen

Date: _____

Dear Parents:

You have participated in a summer orientation to the high school and to our College & Career Center. Now, as part of a total counseling endeavor for freshmen, the Morris High School counselors would like to have a dialogue with you on a variety of topics relevant to your youngsters. The topics will include: student adjustment to a high school; standardized test interpretation; course selection and its ramifications; proper study habits; and college and career planning. The meeting will be held in the auditorium on Tuesday, February 11, at 8:00 P.M. In case of inclement weather, the date will be February 18.

Counselors have already met privately with most of their freshman counselees and are beginning to meet with them again in order to develop their schedule for the next academic year.

We believe that programs like the one forthcoming on February 11 will continue to establish meaningful lines of communication between home and school. We all have the next three and a half years in mind!

We look forward to having you with us.

Sincerely,

_____

Joseph Morgan
Director of Counseling

Notice of Senior Missing Conferences

October 28, 19_____

Dear Mr. and Mrs. _____:

The Counseling Department is in the process of conferring with senior students to discuss post–high school options.

Occasionally, our students have conflicts and are unable to attend their scheduled conferences. I did, however, send for _____ on two separate occasions, but he/she failed to keep both appointments.

It is important that he/she stop by the Counseling Office to make an appointment to see me.

Your support in this matter would be most appreciated. If you have any further questions or concerns, please don't hesitate to contact me.

Sincerely,

_____
Robert Matthews
Counselor

Need for School Records

This uncommon document is especially useful with those students who transfer in to a school at any point in their senior year.

■   ■   ■

MANSFIELD HIGH SCHOOL
COUNSELING DEPARTMENT

I acknowledge that my child, _____, will not be eligible to graduate from Mansfield High School until complete and official records have been received from his/her previous school(s). Any other records, while useful for developing a program of studies, cannot be considered official.

Furthermore, I understand that my child's graduation status will not be determined until such time as official records have been received by the Mansfield High School Counseling Department.

_____
(Parent/Guardian Signature)

School Records Release Form

Almost everyone has some sort of release form that needs to be completed prior to the release of any school records.

■ ■ ■

Dear Parent/Guardian:

School policy stipulates that no student information can be shared with an organization or person without the consent of the affected student (if he/she is at least 18 years of age) or the parent/guardian (if the student is less than 18 years of age). Consequently, until we receive the proper authorized signature(s) on the form below, we cannot send any information to designated persons or organizations.

Name: _____ Graduation Year (if applicable): _____

I hereby grant permission to release my son's/daughter's/my transcript/records to the following person/organization:

Individual/Organization _____

Address _____

_____

_____

Signature of Parent/Guardian

_____

Signature of Adult Student

Invitation to Place Child in Counseling Group

ELEMENTARY SCHOOL COUNSELING NOTES

Date: _____

Dear Parents:

Many of our students have concerns that other youngsters also have. A student can benefit from the opportunity to discuss his or her feelings about these concerns within a counseling group. We are organizing groups comprised of eight students that will meet for forty-five minutes a week for six to eight weeks. Groups are currently being formed to address the following issues:

Death and Bereavement   Stepfamilies

Divorce/Separation   Self-Image Enhancement

If you believe that your child would benefit from exposure to one or more of the topics listed above, please contact me here in the Counseling Office, or notify your child's home-base teacher. We'll be happy to give you more information.

Incidentally, the counseling program here in the lower grades is designed to support students, teachers, *and* parents. May I invite you to get in touch with me if you feel the need to discuss the emotional, social, or scholastic development of your child.

Thank you!

_____

Susan Kingsley
Counselor

Invitation to Program on Divorce/Separation Issues

Date: _____

Dear Parent:

As you know, many of the children in our school are members of a divorced/separated family. We have planned an informative evening program here at the Patrick Duncan School so that we can discuss issues pertaining to different family situations involved in that experience.

If you are separated or divorced, are a member of a stepfamily—or just have close friends or family who are, we invite you to be part of the discussion.

The program will be held twice: on February 1 and on February 2. Both sessions will be held in the Patrick Duncan School library at 7:30 P.M.

Please share this information with your child's other parent. You may both decide to attend, either together or separately.

I look forward to seeing you in February. If you have additional questions, don't hesitate to contact me at 555-2222.

Sincerely,

_____

Helen Dietz
Counselor

· ·

(Please detach and return to your child's teacher by January 25.)

Parent Meeting—Counseling

/_____/ I will attend the February 1, 7:30 P.M. meeting.

/_____/ I will attend the February 2, 7:30 P.M. meeting.

Number of people attending: _____

Your name(s): _____

Child's name: _____

Classroom teacher's name: _____

Notice of Child Abuse Film Screening

Date: _____

Dear Parents:

As part of our child abuse prevention program, we will be showing the film *Now I Can Tell My Secret* in all second-grade classrooms between February 15 and February 20.

The film portrays a nine-year-old boy who resides in a community similar to ours. He is molested by a neighbor and told to keep "their secret."

This well-made film conveys the message of empowerment in a clear manner and reinforces the prevention strategies taught in the Child Abuse Prevention Program (CAP).

There will be a screening of the movie for parents of PS #59 on January 25 at 8:00 P.M. in the school's all-purpose room. You are cordially invited to attend. I will be available that evening to answer any questions that you might have.

If you would like your child excluded from this particular activity, please send a note to Mr. Frank Stanton, principal, by February 10. An appropriate alternative program will be provided for those children not attending the presentation.

Sincerely,

_____

George R. Lyons
Counselor

Parenting Workshop Invitation

The K–8 Counselors of the Dalton Public School District
invite you to a presentation of

WHAT YOU WANTED TO KNOW ABOUT PARENTING
BUT WERE AFRAID TO ASK

at

The Howard Blackman School

on

Tuesday, April 20, 19_____

at

7:30 P.M.

There will be a general meeting from 7:30 (sharp) to 7:45 in the cafeteria, followed by a series of workshops. We hope that you can attend one or two of them.

Please check your workshop choice(s) on the registration form below, and return it to your child's teacher. Thanks!

Name: _____

Child's name: _____

Teacher's name: _____

SUICIDE PREVENTION, presented by Lucille Dougherty and Mark Johnson from the Youth Crisis Center _____ 7:50–9:15

HELPING YOUR CHILD DEAL WITH PEER PRESSURE, presented by Cheryl Cartwright from the Dalton Medical Health Center _____ Session A 7:50–8:30 or _____ Session B 8:40–9:15

HELPING YOUR CHILD BUILD SELF-ESTEEM, presented by Dr. Hans Diedrich, psychologist and family therapist _____ Session A 7:50–8:30 or _____ Session B 8:40–9:15

IMPROVING COMMUNICATION BETWEEN YOU AND YOUR CHILD, presented by Dr. Robert Balsamore, clinical psychologist and family therapist _____ Session A 7:50–8:30 or _____ Session B 8:40–9:15

COPING WITH SINGLE PARENTHOOD, presented by Helene Rigby from the Dalton Mental Health Center _____ Session A 7:50–8:30 or _____ Session B 8:40–9:15

(Refreshments will be served in the cafeteria from 8:15–9:30.)

Reducing Report Card Stress: Workshop Agenda

A child's total effort and achievement during an entire marking period is summed up by a column of letters and/or teacher comments on one or more pieces of paper.

In most cases, children and parents are aware of teacher expectations and how these expectations are being met as the school year progresses. Nonetheless, the issuance of report cards can be an unduly stressful time for an entire family.

This topic has the makings of a meaningful and worthwhile evening workshop for parents of elementary school children. Here is a brief syllabus that can be useful in developing such a workshop.

■   ■   ■

LET'S REDUCE REPORT CARD STRESS

  I. Communication About Academic Progress
    A. As an ongoing process
    B. Special attention to homework and tests
    C. Contacting school authorities
    D. Parent/school partnership activities

  II. Keeping Grade Reporting in Perspective
    A. The importance of praise
    B. Recognizing other aspects of school life
    C. Lauding areas of strength and encouraging further development of those that are weak

  III. The Consequences of Punishment
    A. Examining the issue
    B. The effect on self-esteem
    C. The negatives of "labeling"

  IV. The Underlying Reason(s) for Low Grades
    A. Look to the classroom?
    B. A bid for parent attention?
    C. Distractive elements, such as television or study area?
    D. A sign of a personal problem(s)?

  V. Constructive Advice for the Parent
    A. The low-key technique
    B. Improvement plans

(Reducing Report Card Stress: Workshop Agenda, continued)

    C. Utilizing the professional expertise of school teachers, counselors, and administrators

  VI. Taking the Child for Granted

    A. The pitfalls of doing so

    B. The many positives of continued praise

 VII. Handling Setbacks

    A. Overview of the problem

    B. Techniques for handling setbacks

Notice of Nursing Home Program

THE MACMANUS SCHOOL
ABERWOCKY TOWNSHIP, MN

Date: _____

Dear Parent/Guardian:

As part of our counseling curriculum this academic year, we will be implementing a special sensitivity program for our fourth and fifth graders.

The goals of the program are: to assist youngsters in gaining a more positive attitude toward the elderly; to promote ongoing communication between youngsters and the elderly; and to increase mutual appreciation of the special qualities the youngsters and the elderly have to share.

With these things in mind, our students will visit Meadow Lakes next Wednesday morning. Once at the home, we will converse with the residents, share some songs, and present the residents with various craft and personal items.

We will travel to Meadow Lakes by school bus. Students will be supervised by members of the counseling and teaching staffs.

If you would like to donate such items as hand lotion, combs, tissues, or colognes, have your youngster bring them to school with his or her permission slip.

We thank you for your support and cooperation in this matter.

Sincerely,

_____
Marjorie Springstein
Counselor

Counseling Advisory Committee Meeting

Since counselors are not the sole owners of counseling programs, one of the most effective means of broadening ownership—and at the same time insuring that counselors are doing what they should be doing—is creating a broad-based advisory committee. (Unfortunately, this has occurred in all too few school systems.) The committee usually holds bimonthly evening meetings and can include parents, business leaders, teachers, and counselors. Those districts that have instituted advisory committees find them to be an excellent way to keep "necessary" programs seen as such in the eyes of the community. Here are the minutes of a committee meeting.

■　　■　　■

COUNSELING ADVISORY COMMITTEE MEETING
September 25, 19_____—7:30 P.M.

Minutes

Introductory Remarks	Mr. Stanford reviewed the purpose of the steering committee. He then asked members to introduce themselves and, where appropriate, parents to identify the schools their children attended.
Counseling of Seniors	Mr. Stanford discussed the various aspects of the senior counseling program, which includes the two special evening meetings and the individual senior interview. He reviewed the mechanics of the senior interview for the committee.
Standardized Testing	Mr. Stanford introduced Joyce Barrett, district testing coordinator, who reviewed the standardized testing program at the secondary level, including the new features of the state proficiency examination.
Junior High Counseling	A review was made of individual and group counseling activities at the 7 through 9 level. Mr. Stanford also described the special nondevelopmental summer projects in which secondary school counselors were involved.
November Agenda Item	"The Counselor and the Child Study Team as a Team"
Good of the Cause	Mrs. Harrelson expressed concern that new freshman students are not being seen routinely until the month of

Town Proclamation of National School Counseling Week

What a wonderful way to enhance counselor image in a community! At the time of "National School Counseling Week," ask your local mayor to issue a proclamation.

■   ■   ■

TOWNSHIP OF OCEAN VIEW

John H. Singer
Mayor

PROCLAMATION

WHEREAS, school counselors are employed in public and parochial schools to help students reach their fullest potential as human beings; and

WHEREAS, school counselors are concerned with students being better able to understand themselves, their abilities, strengths, and talents as they relate to career development and awareness; and

WHEREAS, counselors help parents to focus on ways to further the positive educational, personal, and social growth of their children; and

WHEREAS, counselors care about uniting teachers, parents, administrators, special service personnel, and the community to form an effective counseling program for students; and

WHEREAS, counseling is seen as an essential part of the educational process for all students as they adjust to our very complex society.

NOW, THEREFORE, BE IT PROCLAIMED that I, John H. Singer, Mayor of the Township of Ocean View, do hereby proclaim the week of February 4–10, 1990 as "National School Counseling Week."

Given Under My Hand and the Great Seal of the Township of Ocean View this Fifth Day of February in the Year One Thousand Nine Hundred and Ninety and in the Two Hundred Fourteenth Year of Our Nation's Independence.

Mayor John H. Singer

16. EVALUATION AND ACCOUNTABILITY

Much of what a teacher does is visible to even the most casual observer, but individual counseling is like an Arctic iceberg: the tip can be seen, but the mass beneath is invisible. You are seen talking with counselees, but the hours of preconference research and preparation go unnoticed—and so do all the closed-door, nonobservable workings. If you intend to account for yourself, a planned program of evaluation is vital.

Planned evaluation results in objective information on the effectiveness of particular activities, and it can also influence your department when it comes to setting goals. Direct involvement of administrators and/or teachers can be helpful. Today's administrators are interested in enlisting staff support to establish annual building goals. Therefore, asking administrators to share in your research and evaluation program is nothing short of smart politics. Incidentally, *next* year's planning should take place before *this* year's summer break, while things are fresh in everyone's mind and all staff personnel are readily available for input.

In the long run, documentation is the only means of convincing others of program impact. How well counseling programs grow—or if indeed they survive—has a lot to do with how well counselors document the effectiveness of the program *and* their own effectiveness as counselors. It is most beneficial, therefore, to receive constructive criticism on the development of one's counseling skills; but observation by the department supervisor still doesn't happen often enough.

It is important that counselors be personally evaluated by administrators/supervisors by being observed in action. And it's better to be observed and evaluated by an in-house supervisor with a counseling background, than by a down-the-hall administrator with little experience in the counseling process. The most successful counseling programs are those in which the supervisor is knowledgeable, competent, and close.

All too often, though, school counselors are observed or evaluated by standard teacher report forms. This topic contains reporting forms specifically designed to accommodate student services personnel.

Observation Report

OBSERVATION REPORT

School Psychologists, Counselors, Learning Disabilities Specialists, Social Workers, Nurses, and Speech/Language Therapists

Name: _____ Position: _____

School: _____ Evaluator: _____ Date: _____

Information for this report has been derived from the following sources:

E = Exceeds Expectations   M = Meets Expectations   NI = Needs Improvement
NA = Not Applicable   NO = Not Observed

MAJOR ROLE FUNCTIONS   E   M   NI   NA   NO

Professional Demeanor and Ethics

1. Demonstrates and utilizes contemporary, professional knowledge.
2. Attends meetings and conferences, doing so in a timely fashion.
3. Prepares, where necessary, for meetings and conferences.
4. Submits required reports and other documents on time.
5. Maintains confidentiality where appropriate.
6. Demonstrates a high level of professional and ethical conduct.

Assessment/Evaluation

1. Collects and utilizes student information.
2. Selects appropriate evaluation instruments and/or procedures.
3. Administers formal tests/screenings according to recognized standards.
4. Performs noninstrument-based assessment.

(Observation Report, continued)

MAJOR ROLE FUNCTIONS   E M NI NA NO

5. Interprets evaluation/screening data.
6. Integrates this data with findings of other professionals.
7. Documents and disseminates evaluation information properly.

Program Planning

1. Coordinates services with other school buildings, school personnel, and community agencies.
2. Participates in conferences pertinent to students' needs.
3. Takes part in the design of prereferral intervention plans where appropriate.
4. Maintains documentation of prereferral intervention service.

Delivery of Professional Services

1. Assists department in implementing annual goals and objectives.
2. Provides direct professional service to students.
3. After staff consultation, discontinues intervention services when appropriate.
4. Provides consultation services to other staff personnel.

Consultation/Education

1. Promotes awareness of the roles and functions of professional support services staff.
2. Assists with formal/informal in-service education.
3. Encourages the acceptance of students with special needs.
4. Takes part in the individualization and modification of student programs of studies.
5. Serves as a resource on mental and physical health issues.

(Observation Report, continued)

MAJOR ROLE FUNCTIONS   E M NI NA NO

6. Supplies information to staff personnel and local citizenry as to available community resources.

Communication Skills

1. Promotes effective interpersonal relations.
2. Communicates competently in oral and written expression.
3. Encourages effective interdisciplinary relationships.
4. Acts as a liaison to inside/outside agencies and services.

Organization and Program Management

1. Adheres to and helps implement Board of Education and administrative policies/procedures.
2. Abides by building/department policies and procedures.
3. Establishes priorities and appropriate time lines for delivery of services.
4. Manages time efficiently.
5. Maintains required records.
6. Assists in budget planning.
7. Participates in staff development programs and parent education programs.

Summary Evaluation

The follow-through on one or two observations is an end-of-year evaluation. Note that with this particular report form a conference is required. In some school systems, the evaluated professional has the prerogative of waiving such a conference. More importantly, note that the evaluated professional is offered the opportunity to respond in writing to the evaluator's written comments.

■   ■   ■

END-OF-YEAR SUMMARY EVALUATION
SCHOOL YEAR _____

School Psychologists, Counselors, Learning Disabilities Specialists, Social Workers, Nurses, and Speech/Language Therapists

Name: _____ Position: _____

School: _____ Evaluator: _____ Date: _____

PROFESSIONAL DEMEANOR AND ETHICS

Strengths:

Areas in need of improvement:

ASSESSMENT/EVALUATION

Strengths:

Areas in need of improvement:

PROGRAM PLANNING

Strengths:

Areas in need of improvement:

DELIVERY OF PROFESSIONAL SERVICES

Strengths:

Areas in need of improvement:

(Summary Evaluation, continued)

CONSULTATION/EDUCATION

Strengths:

Areas in need of improvement:

COMMUNICATION SKILLS

Strengths:

Areas in need of improvement:

ORGANIZATION AND PROGRAM MANAGEMENT

Strengths:

Areas in need of improvement:

ADDITIONAL COMMENTS:

EVALUATOR'S RECOMMENDATIONS:

COMMENTS BY EVALUATED PROFESSIONAL:

Conference Date _____

Evaluator's Signature _____

Staff Member's Signature _____ Date _____

Program Evaluation

PROGRAM EVALUATION

Dear Parents:

In an effort to assess and thereby improve the effectiveness of this evening's program, we would appreciate it if you would complete this evaluation form. Please circle the appropriate responses.

CODE:	1	2	3	4
	Poor	Adequate	Good	Excellent

1. Manner in which you were informed about this program?

     1   2   3   4

Comments: _____

2. Topics covered during presentation?

     1   2   3   4

Comments: _____

3. The printed material distributed during the session?

     1   2   3   4

4. Your overall reaction to the program?

     1   2   3   4

Comments: _____

A. Should the program be modified in any way for next year? Circle: Y   N

    If yes, in what way? _____

B. Were there any topics not covered?   Y   N

    If yes, what ones? _____

C. Additional Comments: _____

_____

Thank you for sharing your thoughts with us and for attending this evening's meeting.

Student Evaluation of Counselor

STUDENT EVALUATION OF COUNSELING SERVICES

Dear Student:

The Counseling Department continues to seek ways of doing a better job for all students. Your honest answers to the following questions will be studied and then used to improve counseling services. Thank you for taking the time to complete this evaluation form.

Your Name (optional) _____ Class of 19_____

Your Counselor's Name: _____

1. As you spent time with your counselor this year, what aspects of the overall counseling program were the most meaningful and productive? (Examples: selecting and/or changing courses; college and/or career planning; learning about interests, abilities, and values; assistance with academic matters; help with personal problems; etc.)

2. In what ways could your counselor have been more helpful?

3. What recommendations would you make for improving counseling services?

Compensatory Time Record/Request

It has become increasingly common for school systems to grant compensatory time to those counselors who are expected to work beyond the normal school day. Such a program can run the gamut from the chairperson simply saying, "Why don't you take a few hours off," to the more formal negotiated-by-contract arrangement partially reflected in this two-part form. Using part one of the form, the counselor logs in all time earned. The counselor then utilizes part two to request all, or any portion of, the earned time.

■   ■   ■

COMPENSATORY TIME RECORD

Name: _____ Position: _____

Amount of Overtime Worked (hours/minutes):

Date(s): _____ Time: From _____ to _____

_____   _____   _____

_____   _____   _____

Reason: _____

_____

Staff Member Signature _____

Date: _____

REQUEST FOR COMPENSATORY TIME

Name: _____ Position: _____

Amount of Compensatory Time Requested:

Date: _____ Time: From _____ to _____

Staff Member Signature _____

Date: _____

Approved _____ Not Approved _____

Supervisor Signature _____

Date: _____